fresh ALASKA COOKBOOK

BY ROB KINNEEN

PHOTOS BY
ASH ADAMS AND BRIAN ADAMS

Published by
University of Alaska Press
P.O. Box 756240
Fairbanks, AK 99775-6240

Cover and interior design by Jen Gunderson at 590 Design, fiveninetydesign.com
Interior images by Ash Adams and Brian Adams unless otherwise credited.
Cover image by Ash Adams.
Endsheet images of glass balls and tundra by Brian Adams.

Library of Congress Cataloging in Publication Data

Names: Kinneen, Rob, author.
Title: Fresh Alaska cookbook / Rob Kinneen.
Description: Fairbanks, AK : University of Alaska Press, 2018. | Includes index.
Identifiers: LCCN 2018001940 | ISBN 9781602233591 (cloth : alk. paper)
Subjects: LCSH: Cooking, American–Pacific Northwest style. |
Cooking–Alaska. | LCGFT: Cookbooks.
Classification: LCC TX715.2.P32 K55 2018 | DDC 641.5979dc23
LC record available at https://lccn.loc.gov/2018001940

PRINTED IN CANADA

To Carolyn and Sylvie.

To Alaska, her people, her bounty, her beauty.

VII FORAGING

1 INTRODUCTION

7 BITES AND SNACKS

11 Alaska Escabeche with Tzatziki
12 Alaska Seafood Cakes with Apple Slaw
13 Apple Slaw
15 Alaska King Crab Oscar Bites with Béarnaise Aioli
19 Beet and Vodka-Cured Alaska Salmon Gravlax
20 Fresh Rolls with Herring Eggs, Sea Asparagus, Lovage, and Yarrow Dipping Sauce
22 Alaska Oyster Shooter or Granita
23 Alaska Oyster Shooter with Alder-Smoked Salt Rim and Alaskan Summer Ale
23 Roasted Alaska Oysters
25 Alaska Oysters Roasted with Reindeer Sausage and Spinach
27 Muktuk Sushi Roll with Local Bean Sprouts
28 Pan-Seared Alaska Snow Crab–Stuffed Risotto Cakes with Winter Salad
31 Razor Clam Fritters
32 Smoked Salmon White Bean Crostini

35 SOUPS, SIDES, ETC.

36 Arctic Grits or Northern Polenta
38 Corn Soup with Three Sisters Salsa
41 Olive Oil Potatoes
42 Red Wine Barley Risotto
43 Roasted Root Veggies
44 Alaska Salmon Head Pho
48 Sitka Seafood Festival Chowder
49 Dandelion Pesto Potatoes
50 Roasted Garlic Puree
51 Bagna Cauda Vinaigrette
51 Tzatziki
52 Vegetable Stock
52 Crab and Shrimp Stock
53 Fish Stock
53 Chicken Stock

55 BRISTOL BAY

59 SEAFOOD

62 Arctic Shrimp and Grits with Bacon and Red-Eye Gravy
65 Braised Rockfish with Fumet, Vegetables, Seaweed, and Seal Oil
69 Bristol Bay Salmon over Foraged Rice Pasta and Tundra Vinaigrette
72 Clams and Sausage in a White Wine Broth
74 House-Made Salt Cod over Olive Oil Potatoes
75 Pan-Seared Alaska Halibut Cheeks in a Birch–Brown Butter Sauce, served over Alaska Harvest Vegetable Tangle
76 Pan-Seared Scallops with Ras El Hanout and Rosehip Vinaigrette
76 Alaska Rose Hip Vinaigrette
77 Ras El Hanout Spice Blend
78 Salmon with Pickled Beet Vinaigrette and Toasted Quinoa–Root Vegetable Hash
81 Seared Rockfish over Shrimp and Foraged Fried Rice

82 INDIGENIZED CUISINE

89 MEAT AND GAME

90 Coffee-and-Creole-Spiced Reindeer Loin with Spruce-Tip Salt Finish
91 Creole Spice (Bamnation!)
92 Elk Rolled Meatloaf
94 Alaska Game Skewers with Alaska Berry-Birch Syrup Vinaigrette over Fiddleheads and Brown Rice
96 Moroccan-Spiced Umpqua Valley Lamb Chops over Matanuska Valley Carrot Puree and Spruce Tip Syrup
99 Noble's Delight, Featuring Alaska Reindeer
100 Béchamel Sauce
101 Caramelized Onions
102 Red Beans and Rice with Reindeer Sausage
103 Wild Duck Risotto

105 DESSERTS AND BEVERAGES

108 Agudak
110 Fry Bread with Labrador Tea and Cranberries
113 Birch Syrup Crème Brûlée
114 Iced Chaga with Birch Syrup
115 Parsnip Cake with Spruce Tip Crema
116 Rhubarb-Berry Agua Fresca
119 Rhubarb Clafoutis with Whipped Spruce Tip Crema

121 INDEX

127 ACKNOWLEDGMENTS

FORAGING

A word on foraging.

When working with foraged items I always like to start by stating, "I know enough to know I don't know enough about foraging!" This is my blanket statement when working with foraged items.

Knowledge is power—never guess. Even familiar items in different locations can be toxic. Always work in groups and with a knowledgeable individual to cross-check and reference items you are gathering.

Always avoid well-traveled areas. Rinse items well. Some suggest washing in a 4-to-1 vinegar bath and rinsing in plain water after.

Keep in mind that what you are foraging is alive. Don't take more than one-third of the plant you are gathering from. This assures some for others and some for future seasons.

Please be respectful of where you forage, what you forage, and how much you forage.

A great reference in Alaska is *Plants that We Eat* by Anore Jones.

BRIAN ADAMS

INTRODUCTION

I was born and raised in the Last Frontier—on Mitkof Island, in Petersburg, a Southeast Alaska fishing town of 3,000 people. My childhood memories include clamming late at night with my uncles, fishing off the docks, and in the summer picking an endless supply of wild blueberries. I'd carefully place the blueberries into the coffee can held with a string around my neck. I remember anxiously sitting in the captain's cabin of my dad's seining boat, which leaned over almost to the railings when pulling up the nets, full of fish that in my young eyes were almost as big as my father. Playing in the lush forests and muskegs, building forts every day. Family members coming by with smoked fish, shrimp, herring eggs, pickled gumboots—usually to trade for other foods.

We relocated to Nome for a year in elementary school. There, just south of the Arctic Circle, the landscape was vastly different—sparse trees and rolling hills. The foods were different too. I remember being introduced to *agudak* (Eskimo ice cream), a mixture of berries, sugar, and some combination of Crisco, fish, or animal fat. After-school activities consisted of ivory-carving classes, hustling newspapers for the *Nome Nugget* on Thursdays, and finding glass rocks on the beach. The first summer during the Midnight Sun Festival, I recall doing the blanket toss, which scared the bejesus out of me! The toss was traditionally a way for Iñupiat hunters to spot animals across the tundra as the men were tossed in the air and caught on the way down on a walrus-skin hide.

We settled in Anchorage, the biggest city in Alaska, located in the Southcentral region. I took to kitchens, dishwashing and prepping, and will forever be thankful for the culinary arts class I took at the King Career Center. My instructors, Glenn Denkler and Clarence Davis, set me on my path to culinary school.

After graduation, I attended the Culinary Institute of America. Gaining experience, I cooked in New Orleans at Emeril Lagasse's NOLA and later in Durham, North Carolina. These places had a sense

BRIAN ADAMS

of food culture that embraced farming, seasonality, and indigenous or ethnic influences. Once I was exposed to the undeniable difference of eating just-picked greens, locally cured meats, seafood right out of the water, and local cheese or ice cream, it was really hard to forget. Years later, searching for these gems would be my inspiration on foraging trips around Alaska. For me, the highlights of traveling are always the celebrations of local flavors.

Returning to Alaska after those experiences, I was determined to dig deeper into local foods. Local food has many different meanings for me, however. From my perspective as a chef working with contemporary foods, it's what you serve from certified ranchers, fishmongers, farmers, and purveyors. It's food that you would find in high-quality restaurants and marketplaces.

Alaska traditional or subsistence foods, meanwhile, are foods that are foraged, gathered, or hunted and processed in homes, with wildly different interpretations across the southeast, southwest, interior, or

BRIAN ADAMS

Arctic parts of the state. Focusing on foraging puts one in touch with the inherent seasonality and environment in Alaska.

Alaska is a very rich and diverse place, full of drastic contrasts between our rainforest, subarctic, and Arctic regions. Geographically the largest state in the union, we are home to just 750,000 residents, nearly half of whom live in Anchorage. There are many villages that are home to just a few hundred people and accessible only by boat or plane.

In the interior and northern regions, temperatures have been known to reach 100°F, with eighteen to twenty-four hours of sunlight, but in the winter they also regularly experience −60°F and just three to four hours of light.

Alaskans are very protective of our resources. We have the only wild sustainable fishery in the nation, and we have fought to preserve it.

The people of Alaska are diverse in their own right—our history includes explorers from all over the world, gold rush miners and profiteers, a vibrant fishing industry, and recent military-industrial influences. Even among our indigenous people, there are five major tribal groups with dozens of languages and largely varying traditions. We are an ancient place with a human history of over 10,000 years, but have been a US state for less than sixty years. You can still discuss the signing of the state constitution and drafting of the Alaska Native Claims Settlement Act with many who were there to experience it.

This contrast translates into what we eat. We look to modern conveniences but hold on to traditions. We actively remember the past but embrace technology that can work for us. There are exciting things happening all across the Last Frontier. This is a taste of what I have found.

BRIAN ADAMS

BITES AND SNACKS

Produce has some very diverse interpretations around the state of Alaska.

The New Deal put a small community on the map in 1945, when FDR sent Midwestern farm families to Palmer, Alaska, in an effort to kick-start farming in the Last Frontier. Long winters and short growing seasons got things off to a rough start. Today, however, we have many farmers in the Matanuska Valley who are prosperous with lettuces, hearty rootstock beets, turnips, squash, and potatoes—lots of potatoes. There are also seasonal dainties as well—peppers, eggplants, and microgreens from hothouses.

In southwestern Bethel, Tim Meyers serves up the usual suspects from soil that used to be a riverbed, kept rich with ground-up fish fertilizer, which explains why he is averaging 100,000 pounds of produce per year—and with a lofty goal of twice that. He already exports produce all around the state and runs his market year-round, selling the bumper crops of root vegetables that he cellars.

In Southeast, the Sitka Farmers Market serves up pickled kelp and devil's club tea, among other uniquely Alaska items. There are two you-pick farms, community plots of land, and a bit of foraging—seaweed, beach asparagus, different berries, spruce tips, and more.

Across Cook Inlet from Alaska's largest city of Anchorage is the 200-person village of Tyonek. The village is thirty minutes by plane but really seems a world away. In 2009, the village council decided to take

Tyonek irrigation system for the community farm. The solar power creates energy for the pump from a nearby lake. ROB KINNEEN

Landing in Tyonek (population 190) in a Cessna from Spernack Airlines. The airport is a maintained gravel airstrip. ROB KINNEEN

food security seriously and started a public garden. This has grown into an operation fueled by a solar power generator for transferring water and also includes two hoop houses and three plots. The garden focuses on natural solutions for pesticides, with seeds planted by elementary school students. Buy-in from these students is important—which is why they are actually growing corn and watermelon! The Tyonek garden supplies Elders with fresh food, offers the community produce at below-market rates, and has created jobs.

Produce is not as easily available in Alaska's northern regions, where diets are based on game meat. These free-roaming animals' own diets consist of nutrient-rich roots, bark, and other dormant plants in the long winter months, providing a diversification of nutrients not found in contemporary USDA farm-raised animals.

Most farmers markets in Alaska start in May and last until October with produce being available in mid to late June. In the event you are foraging for botanicals across the state, success will depend on elevation, geographic location, and environment. For example, berries found at ground level in Southeast in early June can still be blooming in early July at higher elevations or in cooler parts of the state.

One of my favorite Alaska produce stories is one of "Tlingit potatoes." The Tlingit people have always been savvy traders, and one particular strain of potato found in Juneau and small towns in Southeast Alaska has been speculated to have origins as far away as Mexico and Chile.

Tyonek Airport storage building. Artwork depicts Dena'ina Athabascan name for the village—The Beach People. ROB KINNEEN

A visit to Meyer Farms to witness the cold-weather farming techniques he is using to grow 100,000 pounds of vegetables on the tundra. ROB KINNEEN

ASH AD

ALASKA ESCABECHE WITH TZATZIKI

MAKES 6 TO 8 SERVINGS

Escabeche is blanched-marinated seafood, as opposed to ceviche, which is citrus-cured seafood. This is a great way to use the odds and ends of fish after you cut them into portions, which is precisely what restaurants do. This recipe makes two and a half pounds of escabeche.

INGREDIENTS

- 3 tablespoons cooking oil
- ½ red onion, cut julienne
- 2 multicolored bell peppers, cut julienne, or 1 cup sweet chili peppers, cut into rings
- 1 clove garlic, minced
- 1 jalapeño, seeded and minced
- 1 teaspoon red pepper flakes
- 2 oranges, zest and juice
- 2 limes, zest and juice
- 6 cups fumet or fish stock
- 1 pound salmon pieces cut into 1-inch cubes
- 1 pound halibut, rockfish, or cod cut into 1-inch cubes
- 1 tablespoon chopped fresh thyme
- 1 tablespoon chopped fresh oregano
- 1 tablespoon chopped fresh parsley
- 6 to 8 pita, warmed
- 4 to 6 ounces mixed greens
- 2 cups (¼ cup per) tzatziki (see recipe page 51)

PROCEDURE

1. In a sauté pan over medium-high heat, add oil, then onion and peppers. Cook for 1 to 1½ minutes, and then reduce heat if necessary.
2. Add garlic and jalapeño, and cook until the aroma of garlic is apparent, typically 45 seconds.
3. Deglaze with ½ cup orange juice. Pour off into a baking pan and let cool.
4. In a pot, bring the fish stock to a simmer.
5. Cook the fish in batches in the pot, so as not to crowd or crumble.
6. Cook fish for 3 to 4 minutes. Gently remove and add to baking pan with vegetables.
7. When all the fish is cooked and transferred to the baking pan, cover with remaining citrus juice and zest, and sprinkle with salt.
8. Refrigerate until cool, then finish with herbs and gently mix so you do not break up the fish too much.
9. Serve on warm pita with mixed greens and tzatziki.

Keeps for up to two or three days.

ALASKA SEAFOOD CAKES WITH APPLE SLAW

MAKES 16 2-OUNCE PORTIONS

This recipe has produced welcome responses and empty plates. People really enjoy the chockfull-of-seafood flavor and texture of these seafood cakes!

My personal favorite fishmonger, Anchorage's Favco, highlights Bristol Bay sockeye salmon, mixed with Alaska whitefish (cod or rockfish), for a terrific result. It is becoming more common for seafood companies to provide pouches of seafood with spoon meat (the meat from between the spine and rib cage), tails, collars, and bellies in one- and three-pound packages.

Serve over apple slaw, as the tartness of the apples and vinegar hold up nicely to the rich seafood.

INGREDIENTS FOR SEAFOOD CAKES

- 2 cloves garlic, minced
- ½ cup finely diced celery
- ½ cup finely diced red onion
- 2 tablespoons Dijon mustard
- 1 tablespoon Creole seasoning
- 1 teaspoon Worcestershire sauce
- 1 teaspoon Tabasco
- 2 eggs
- 1 pound salmon chunks or ground salmon, lightly pressed to remove excess moisture (yields 12 ounces)
- 1 pound cod or rockfish chunks, lightly pressed to remove excess moisture (yields about 14 ounces)
- ½ cup panko

Use whatever type of fish you have on hand; the idea here is total utilization of seafood.

For a gluten-free version, use rice or crumbled corn cereal, or gluten-free breadcrumbs. Be sure the package label says "Gluten Free."

PROCEDURE FOR SEAFOOD CAKES

1. Preheat oven to 375°F.
2. Line a nonstick cookie sheet with parchment paper.
3. Combine garlic, celery, onion, mustard, Creole seasoning, Worcestershire sauce, Tabasco sauce, and eggs in a bowl.
4. Add the seafood and mix thoroughly.
5. Add panko sparingly—just enough to bind the seafood mixture.
6. Form into desired-sized patties and place on cookie sheet.
7. Bake for 8 minutes.
8. Check for doneness. Cakes should feel firm on the outside with a cooked golden crust.

ASH ADAMS

APPLE SLAW

MAKES 4 TO 6 SERVINGS

As a child, I was traumatized by my dad's aggressive use of mayonnaise in sandwiches and salad preparations. Sorry, RJK1. BLT fixings were known to slide out uncontrollably during lunch; it was a difficult time in my life.

Imagine my delight when I came across this vinegar-based slaw dressing! It was tart, sweet, and floral, and with a nice crunch. Over the past few years Alaska has been trying to make a go of it with apples, and there have even been successful years, when the crabapple grafts have produced nice juicy apples bigger than a golf ball! Those are quite nice and do this dressing justice.

INGREDIENTS

⅓ cup champagne vinegar

¼ cup Dijon mustard

2 tablespoons honey or birch syrup

1 cup olive oil

2 apples, shredded, skins on

½ red onion, julienne

3 leaves basil, julienne

½ head red or green cabbage, shaved with a kitchen mandoline or julienne

PROCEDURE

1. With an immersion stick or a blender, mix the vinegar, Dijon mustard, and honey. Once mixed well, slowly add the oil into the base and emulsify.
2. Add the shredded apple, red onions, and basil.
3. For best results, mix the dressing with the cabbage 15 minutes before serving. This keeps the slaw crisp and sweet.
4. Keep extra dressing in glass jar for later use.

ASH ADAMS

ALASKA KING CRAB OSCAR BITES WITH BÉARNAISE AIOLI

MAKES 10 SERVINGS

I made this as an appetizer for the release of *For the Rights of All: Ending Jim Crow in Alaska*, a 2009 documentary film about twentieth-century Alaska Native struggles for civil and land rights.

The premiere occurred at the National Museum of the American Indian in Washington, DC, a trip that had a big influence on me personally and professionally. Our crab came from the Norton Sound Economic Development Corporation, where cold, shallow waters produce a smaller king crab that is unbelievably tender and sweet.

INGREDIENTS FOR ALASKA CRAB OSCAR BITES

10 ounces beef tenderloin, cut into 1-inch cubes

6 ounces Alaska king crab, shelled and cut into 1-inch pieces

¼ pound asparagus

Salt and pepper

Translucent skewers

PROCEDURE FOR ALASKA CRAB OSCAR BITES

1. In boiling water, blanch asparagus and plunge into an ice bath to stop cooking. Cut on the bias into half-inch pieces.
2. Season the cubed beef with salt and pepper, then sear on each side over medium heat until medium rare, or to your preferred doneness. Set aside to cool.
3. Clean crab to ensure that there is no remaining cartilage in the leg meat.

INGREDIENTS FOR REDUCTION

1 ounce minced small shallot

½ cup champagne vinegar

2 sprigs fresh tarragon (reserve half for garnish, chop remaining)

PROCEDURE FOR REDUCTION

1. In a small saucepan, combine champagne vinegar and and shallots over medium-high heat. Reduce until just a fourth of the original amount remains.
2. Allow reduction to cool, and then add to the aioli.
3. Fold in tarragon.

Alaska King Crab Oscar Bites with Béarnaise Aioli (cont.)

INGREDIENTS FOR BÉARNAISE AIOLI

2 egg yolks
½ teaspoon minced garlic
½ teaspoon Dijon mustard
3 tablespoons apple cider vinegar
¾ cup olive oil
Salt to taste

PROCEDURE FOR BÉARNAISE AIOLI

1. Add the egg yolks, garlic, Dijon mustard, and vinegar to a mixing bowl. Whisk until it is a pale yellow color and fully incorporated.
2. Slowly begin adding the oil to the mix, drizzling consistently while whisking and making sure to incorporate.
3. Add salt to taste and fold in the cooled reduction to finish sauce.

ASSEMBLY PROCEDURE

1. Using a translucent skewer, stab one piece of seared beef, then three or four pieces of asparagus, and complete with a piece of crab.
2. Garnish with a dollop of aioli and tarragon.
3. Repeat until you have used up all ingredients.

ASH ADAMS

BEET AND VODKA-CURED ALASKA SALMON GRAVLAX

MAKES 3 POUNDS (ABOUT 48 1-OUNCE SERVINGS)

In 2015, I was asked to assist with some Alaska-inspired recipes in a partnership between Princess Cruises and the Alaska Seafood Marketing Institute. This included traveling to Juneau and Ketchikan to cook these dishes for the executive crew of the cruise ships when they were at dock. These ships can hold up to 4,000 passengers. They are truly like floating towns or little worlds. It was amazing to be behind the scenes on these vessels.

Alaska's abundance of beets and vodka was my inspiration to showcase this cured gravlax. Alaska distilleries have made a big splash in the last few years, using unique Alaska ingredients like glacial ice, smoked salmon (really!), rhubarb, and Alaska-grown grains and potatoes. Additionally, you can confidently find Alaska beets all year long in the Last Frontier. I enjoy the bright red hue and earthy flavor the beets lend to the salmon in this dish.

For additional fun, try this with a white king salmon!

INGREDIENTS

- 5 pounds salmon, skin on and pin-boned
- 5 sprigs thyme, roughly chopped
- ⅓ cup brown sugar
- ⅓ cup granulated sugar
- ½ cup kosher salt
- ¼ cup lemon zest
- ½ cup grated fresh red beet
- ½ cup vodka (preferably from an Alaska distillery)

PROCEDURE

1. In a small bowl, mix sugars, salt, herbs, and lemon zest.
2. Place the salmon fillets, flesh side up, on a flat surface covered with wide plastic wrap.
3. Spread vodka evenly over salmon fillets.
4. Spread the grated beet evenly over the fillets.
5. Distribute the sugar/salt mixture evenly over the fillets.
6. Wrap the plastic wrap securely around the salmon so that it makes an airtight package. This may take some trial and error.
7. Place the salmon in a large-sided pan and turn the wrapped salmon over every day for four days. To expedite the process, place another large pan on top of the salmon to weigh it down. You can also use several evenly distributed canned foods for a day or two. Keep refrigerated.
8. The fish is cured when the flesh bounces back when you poke it with your finger.
9. Lightly rinse the cure off the fillets and wrap them again, tightly, in plastic wrap. If you are not eating them in the next four days, freeze until use.

FRESH ROLLS WITH HERRING EGGS, SEA ASPARAGUS, LOVAGE AND YARROW DIPPING SAUCE

MAKES 1 SERVING

When I started working with indigenous ingredients, it was important to craft menus that were informative and health conscious. Traditional Alaska foods are picked or harvested close to the source. This leads to very high nutritional value, and the idea is to maximize nutritional value by keeping recipes relatively free of gluten, dairy, and alcohol.

Another standard is to make sure ingredients are accessible and not too delicate when visiting remote locations. It is amazing to think about barges offloading seasonally before sea ice sets, which makes many communities accessible during winter only by plane. Lettuce can make the journey from California, only to be frozen and ruined in –40°F weather in Barrow or Fairbanks. Smaller communities might have only one general store. When cooking in remote locations, I like to work around what is locally available.

This recipe has been recreated in Barrow with muktuk (frozen whale skin and blubber) and in Ketchikan with salmon, beach asparagus, and lovage. The idea is to celebrate the place you're from while using what you have. When using this recipe for demonstrations, I love to set it up and have participants make their own—a fresh roll party is the way to go. Even if it does not work, you still have a salad!

INGREDIENTS FOR FRESH ROLLS

1 sheet rice paper

2 berry or squash blossoms (if available) or use fresh herbs

¼ ounce herring eggs or salmon roe

¼ ounce canned or frozen sea asparagus or thinly sliced fresh asparagus

¼ ounce carrots, julienne cut on mandoline

¼ ounce celery, julienne cut on mandoline

½ ounce rice noodles, cooked and cooled

1 leaf romaine lettuce cut lengthwise into thirds

PROCEDURE FOR FRESH ROLLS

1. Bloom the rice paper in lukewarm water to soften. Place on a clean cutting board.
2. When making these, be sure to stack everything in the center of the rice paper. A little goes a long way, so have light hands. Stack according to the ingredients list, so the blossoms or other items on the bottom will showcase nicely.
3. When items are stacked, fold the rice paper like a burrito—top and bottom in first, and fold over from the side. Make sure to keep it tight with pressure.

INGREDIENTS FOR DIPPING SAUCE

¼ cup soy sauce

¼ cup rice vinegar

1 tablespoon brown sugar

½ teaspoon lemon zest

¼ cup lemon juice or juice of one lemon

¼ teaspoon red pepper flakes

2 tablespoons chopped lovage and/or yarrow (or substitute green tea)

PROCEDURE FOR DIPPING SAUCE

1. Mix all ingredients, then set aside.

PROCEDURE FOR PLATING

1. Place the dipping sauce in the center of a platter, with the rolls surrounding it.
2. For best results, brush rolls lightly with oil to keep them from sticking, or use a damp paper towel to store in refrigerator.

HAA AANI OYSTERS FOUR WAYS

In 2012, I was the chef for the inaugural Haa Aani Oysterfest in Juneau. Translating to "Our Land" in Tlingit, Haa Aani is a subsidiary of the Sealaska Corporation meant to preserve livelihoods and create economies in rural Southeast Alaska using natural resources from the environment, which is how the Tlingit people prospered for centuries.

Oysters are not indigenous to Alaska, but the waters are great for cultivating them. Oysterfest was a premiere celebration to highlight bringing the oysters to market after a three-year incubation. Juneau was particularly busy that weekend, as Sealaska's Celebration was in full effect. Celebration is the largest gathering of southeastern indigenous Alaskans, with Tlingit, Haida, and Tsimshian in full regalia. It was soul-filling to see these traditions in full effect, with a glimmer of future traditions being born.

ALASKA OYSTER SHOOTER OR GRANITA

INGREDIENTS

6 Alaska oysters
1 cup water
⅓ cup brown sugar
1 tablespoon minced ginger
½ cup finely diced rhubarb
1 lemon, zested and juiced (or ¼ cup lemon juice)

PROCEDURE

1. Bring water and sugar to a boil.
2. Add ginger and cook for 30 seconds.
3. Add rhubarb, cook for 30 seconds, and remove from heat.
4. Add lemon juice and zest.
5. For granita, pour onto a rimmed cookie sheet and then place in the freezer. Scrape with a fork every 20 minutes until frozen. For a shooter, wait until the ginger-rhubarb water is cool, Add to a shot glass with oyster and cold rhubarb-ginger water.
7. To serve, shuck oysters on the half shell and top each with rhubarb-ginger water or rhubarb granita.

ALASKA OYSTER SHOOTER WITH ALDER-SMOKED SALT RIM AND ALASKAN SUMMER ALE

INGREDIENTS

¼ cup finely diced and seeded cucumber

¼ cup finely diced and seeded tomato

¼ cup finely diced red pepper

6 Alaska oysters

1 lemon wedge

2 teaspoons ground Alaska Pure Sea Salt, alder flavor

1 tablespoon chopped cilantro

1 bottle Alaskan Brewing Company Alaskan Summer Ale

6 shot glasses

PROCEDURE

1. Dice all vegetables and set aside.
2. Shuck oysters.
3. Rub rim of shot glasses with lemon wedge; roll in ground sea salt.
4. Place 1 oyster in each glass, and top with ½ teaspoon of each vegetable and ¼ teaspoon cilantro.
5. Top with 2 teaspoons of Alaskan Brewing Company Alaskan Summer Ale.
6. Shoot 'em and enjoy!

ROASTED ALASKA OYSTERS

INGREDIENTS

1 dozen Alaska oysters, not shucked

½ of a 3-pound box of kosher salt

1 lemon

High-quality cocktail sauce or horseradish

PROCEDURE

1. Preheat oven to 450°F.
2. On a baking pan, spread out kosher salt and lay out the oysters, cup side down, to keep the liquid in after they open.
3. Roast for 10 to 12 minutes, depending on the size, until they open.
4. Remove carefully from oven and dress with a squeeze of lemon, cocktail sauce, or horseradish.

Oysters can be cooked on a medium-hot grill as well, laid cup side down, in between the grates. Cover until they open.

Please note that due to the size of Alaska oysters, the shells are heavy and you may have to double-check that the shells have released. They may not lift up after opening.

ASH A

ALASKA OYSTERS ROASTED WITH REINDEER SAUSAGE AND SPINACH

INGREDIENTS

6 Alaska oysters, shucked on the half shell

4 tablespoons butter

¼ cup finely chopped reindeer sausage* (recommended: Indian Valley Meats mild Polish reindeer sausage)

½ clove garlic, minced

¼ cup lemon juice

1 teaspoon Tabasco

1 cup spinach, cooked, pressed, and chopped

⅓ cup panko

¼ cup grated Parmesan cheese

Salt and pepper

2 tablespoons olive oil, to finish

**You can substitute chorizo for reindeer sausage.*

PROCEDURE

1. Preheat oven to 450°F.
2. Melt butter over medium heat in a sauté pan, then add reindeer sausage.
3. When sausage is crisp, add garlic. Cook for 30 seconds and remove from heat.
4. Add lemon juice and Tabasco.
5. Mix in spinach.
6. Finish with panko and cheese.
7. If the mixture looks dry, add olive oil to finish.
8. Place oysters on a sheet pan, and top each oyster with a heaping tablespoon of the reindeer sausage mixture. Bake for 10 to 12 minutes.

ASH AD

MUKTUK SUSHI ROLL WITH LOCAL BEAN SPROUTS

MAKES 4 ROLLS

In Utqiaġvik (Barrow), a 4,500-person community on the coast of the Arctic Ocean, the sun goes down in late November and doesn't fully return until late January. During that part of the year, the days are like sunsets and at their shortest times are around four hours long. On a visit there in January, we went sightseeing in –40°F!

The Week of Healthy Living is an event sponsored by the local hospital's diabetes prevention program and the local college cooperative extension that promotes positive changes with the return of the sun. There is a walking loop with mini clinics including yoga, essential oils, Zumba, as well as games and food demonstrations.

The first year, while prepping at a local clinic, I had my electric hot top, a pot, a pan, and a cutting board and knives I brought with me. The excitement of preparing foods in new locations never gets old. I love unfolding the logistics to make the best situation possible.

This sushi dish highlights a local food called muktuk, which is the fat of a whale, in a different light. Muktuk is rich in omega-3 fatty acids and other trace minerals. The nori is rich in vitamin A and other trace minerals, helping absorb the omega-3 fatty acids into your system, compensating for lack of sunlight.

INGREDIENTS FOR THE RICE

2 cups sushi (short-grain) rice

2 cups water

2 tablespoons sugar

2 tablespoons rice wine vinegar

1 tablespoon salt

PROCEDURE FOR RICE

1. Rinse the rice three times, or until the water runs clear.
2. In a pot, bring water to a boil. Add rice, stir, cover, and let cook on low for 15 minutes.
3. Let rice sit for another 10 minutes with the heat off.
4. In a glass bowl, spread rice out, and fold in sugar, salt, and vinegar. Set aside.

INGREDIENTS FOR THE SUSHI

Nori seaweed paper

Cooked sushi rice

1 carrot, julienne (matchstick size)

1 cucumber, julienne (matchstick size)

½ cup mung bean sprouts (in Alaska, use Alaska sprouts!)

Muktuk (or smoked salmon), sliced thin

1 bunch sea asparagus

PROCEDURE FOR SUSHI

1. Place nori shiny side down.
2. Place about ¾ cup of cooked rice on the nori.
3. Spread rice out evenly over the nori. Be sure to leave about a half-inch on each end to complete the roll.
4. In the center of the roll, place carrot, sea asparagus, cucumber, sprouts, and muktuk. Use ½ to ¾ ounce per ingredient.
5. Roll rice, being sure to keep ingredients in the center and applying pressure to the nori.
6. Cut the roll in half, then each half into fourths. A roll should make 8 pieces.
7. Serve with wasabi or soy sauce. For a gluten-free option, serve with tamari.

Helpful Hint: When spreading rice on nori, keep a little bowl of water for dipping your fingers, so the rice does not stick to your fingers.

PAN-SEARED ALASKA SNOW CRAB–STUFFED RISOTTO CAKES WITH WINTER SALAD

MAKES 8 2-OUNCE CAKES

This recipe was my contribution to James Fraioli's *Wild Alaskan Seafood* book. My recipe uses the humble snow crab, and its unique texture and subtle sweetness is really quite satisfying. It pairs up well with the risotto and the crisp snap of the winter vegetables.

INGREDIENTS FOR RISOTTO CAKES

¼ cup olive oil
¼ cup finely diced onion
¼ cup finely diced celery
1 clove garlic, minced
1 cup Arborio rice
½ cup white wine
3 cups fresh crab stock (see Crab and Shrimp stock recipe on page 52)
⅓ ounce salt
1 teaspoon pepper
8 ounces shelled snow crab
⅓ cup semolina flour
1 cup cooking oil for frying

PROCEDURE FOR RISOTTO CAKES

1. In a stockpot over medium heat, add olive oil, garlic, onion, and celery. Cook until translucent and avoid browning.
2. Add Arborio rice, stirring continuously to coat the rice evenly.
3. Deglaze with wine and keep stirring.
4. When the wine has been incorporated with the rice, add one cup of the crab stock. Stir continuously.
5. When stock has been absorbed, add another cup of stock, stirring.
6. With the last cup, be sure to taste the rice. It should be cooked through but still toothy, as it is going to continue cooking while it rests. Make sure the pearl of the rice is cooked through. If the pearl is not cooked through, it will taste gritty.
7. Finish with salt and pepper to taste.
8. When the risotto is firm to the bite but cooked through and the liquid has been absorbed, spread the risotto out onto a pan to cool.
9. When cool enough to handle, form the risotto into 2-inch round balls.
10. With your thumb, make a divot and add in about 1 ounce of crab.
11. Reform the ball, then flatten it out into a cake that is thin enough to pan fry.
12. Dust each cake with semolina flour.
13. In a medium-size sauté pan, begin to heat ½ inch of oil. Check the temperature of the oil by dropping a small piece of rice into the pan; it should sizzle.
14. Gently place the cakes into the hot oil, cooking approximately 1 minute per side as they should not get too dark. Remove to a plate lined with paper towels.
15. Season with salt and pepper.

INGREDIENTS FOR WINTER SALAD

1 small fennel bulb, shaved thin

1 small granny smith apple, julienne

½ celery root with outer skin removed, thin julienne

1 lemon, juiced

2 tablespoons chopped parsley, or use the chopped fronds from the fennel bulb

1 tablespoon birch syrup

¼ cup vegetable oil

Salt and pepper

PROCEDURE FOR WINTER SALAD

1. Toss the shaved fennel bulb, apple, and celery root together.
2. In a separate mixing bowl, combine the lemon juice and parsley, then drizzle in the birch syrup and oil.
3. Toss and arrange salad over two risotto cakes per plate.

ASH AD

RAZOR CLAM FRITTERS

MAKES 6 TO 8 SERVINGS

When I lived in North Carolina, I would call the fishmonger to inquire about what was fresh and available. The fish we received was typically less than twenty-four hours out of the ocean.

In Alaska, the 33,000 miles of coastline seldom meet up with the road system. Due to this circumstance and higher-quality refrigeration standards, it's rare to find fresh scallops or razor clams. Please use not only the shucked cleaned meat but the residual or thawed juice from the clam as well. The rich clam meat and chew of the fritter compliments the cool, refreshing acidic dollop of tzatziki (see page 51 for recipe). Enjoy!

INGREDIENTS

2 cups all-purpose flour

2 teaspoons baking powder

1 teaspoon iodized salt

¼ teaspoon black pepper

2 eggs, beaten

1 tablespoon unsalted butter

Milk and clam juice to make ½ cup total

1 pound frozen razor clams

FRITTER PROCEDURE

1. Mix the flour, baking soda, salt, and pepper. Sift once to incorporate thoroughly.
2. Mix the wet ingredients: Beat the eggs, mix in milk/clam juice combo, and add in minced clams.
3. Fold the dry ingredients into the wet, one third at a time.
4. Scoop 1 ounce of the mixture at a time and fry in 375°F fryer.

For griddle cakes: add ¼ ounce milk to the recipe. Then, in a medium-gauge pan over medium heat melt a tablespoon of unsalted butter and add the batter. When the bottom of the cake firms and you see the batter turning more doughy, flip. Cook for a minute. For best results make them a 50-cent piece size and serve as an appetizer.

SMOKED SALMON WHITE BEAN CROSTINI

MAKES 6 TO 8 SERVINGS

This recipe was developed to highlight a smoked salmon dish not knee-deep in mayonnaise, cream cheese, or sour cream. It works for both smoked salmon and leftover salmon cooked the previous night.

During the Native Youth Olympics in Anchorage, families from all over the state visit our biggest city to compete in traditional Native games. A side attraction is a recipe competition, with a first prize of a year's supply of pilot bread crackers. Alaska is the foremost consumer of these hardtack gems, and you can find them in the most remote villages. I like to use them in moderation when working with traditional foods.

INGREDIENTS

15-ounce can white beans, reserve 2 ounces juice

1 lemon, juice and zest for 1 teaspoon zest and 2 ounces juice

1 tablespoon chopped fresh parsley

6 ounces smoked salmon, skin off, chunked into large pieces

Salt and pepper, fresh cracked

Sailor Boy crackers

PROCEDURE

1. Rinse the white beans and put into a medium-size bowl.
2. Chop and smash the beans with a fork or sturdy whisk.
3. Stir in the lemon juice and zest, and add bean juice.
4. Stir in the chopped parsley.
5. Fold the smoked salmon chunks into the bean mixture until well mixed.
6. Serve on Sailor Boy crackers.

BRIAN ADAMS

SOUPS, SIDES, ETC.

ARCTIC GRITS OR NORTHERN POLENTA

MAKES 2 TO 4 SERVINGS

Bryce and Jan Wrigley moved to Delta Junction, Alaska, in 1983. In 2011 they started the Alaska Flour Company, creating the only flour mill in Alaska. Adhering to environmental and stewardship practices to protect the environment and maintain a quality product, their main inspiration was to create a local food infrastructure in a remote state that imports 96 percent of its food.

Alaska Flour's product line is ever-expanding: whole hulled barley, barley flour, barley cereal, toasted barley tea, barley couscous, and cookie, brownie, and pancake mixes. Watch out, world!

I have made it my business to support those creating food in Alaska. Sometimes this means buying items and working around them to develop recipes. Working in North Carolina and New Orleans was the inspiration for finishing this barley breakfast cereal in a savory fashion.

Where we may fall short on formal traditional food recipes, we can create new recipes and traditions based on our experiences.

INGREDIENTS

1 tablespoon vegetable oil
1 clove garlic, sliced thin
½ shallot, sliced into rings
⅛ teaspoon red pepper flakes
½ cup white wine
2 cups vegetable stock
½ cup Alaska Flour Cream of Barley Breakfast Cereal
½ cup cream
2 tablespoons unsalted butter
1 tablespoon grated Parmesan cheese
1 teaspoon chopped fresh sage
1 teaspoon chopped fresh thyme
Salt and pepper to taste

PROCEDURE

1. In a medium-size saucepan, preferably stainless steel with a thick-gauge bottom, heat to medium-high and add oil, garlic, and shallot. Let them sweat.
2. When the garlic and shallots are fragrant, and the shallots look lightly toasted or glassy, add the red pepper flakes and wine.
3. When the mixture comes to a boil, add the stock and bring back to boiling.
4. At the boil, add the barley, stirring consistently with a whisk. Keep it moving until you notice the barley blooming, creating a thicker mush.
5. As the barley cooks, turn the heat to a simmer or low heat and keep stirring until you can taste no rawness or texture on the barley cereal. Add a touch of water if needed to keep it from becoming too thick.
6. Fold in the cream.
7. When the cream is incorporated, turn off the heat and fold in the cheese, butter, and herbs.

ASH ADAMS

ASH ADAMS

CORN SOUP WITH THREE SISTERS SALSA

MAKES 4 SERVINGS

I made this soup for the 2012 National Indian Health Board's awards gala in Denver, Colorado. It creates a dialog of the Three Sisters: corn, beans, and squash. The corn provides structure for the growing beans and shade for the squash. The beans attract nitrogen for sturdy roots, essential for all three.

Nutritionally, the beans provide protein, the corn is packed with carbohydrates, and the squash has essential vitamins, found in the fruit of the flesh, and essential oils from the seeds. At the end of a season, the plants go to seed and leave the environment as good as or better than it was before. Native Americans practiced this regenerative way of planting for centuries. This soup is a reminder of the importance of listening to your environment and respecting the past.

When cooking with and/or for indigenous populations, I typically keep health in mind. There is no alcohol or cream in this soup. The olive oil provides the richness and viscous mouth feel. I guarantee no one will notice this is a vegan soup!

INGREDIENTS FOR CORN SOUP

2 tablespoons canola oil
½ onion, diced
½ stalk celery, diced
1 cup apple juice
1 clove garlic, minced
1 cup corn kernels (fresh or frozen)
2 cups vegetable stock
6 tablespoons olive oil
Salt and pepper

PROCEDURE FOR CORN SOUP

1. Heat vegetable oil in a pot over medium heat. Add onion and celery.
2. When the onion and celery begin to sweat, add garlic and apple juice. Continue cooking until the liquid has reduced by half.
3. Add the corn and vegetable stock. Bring to a boil.
4. Puree with an immersion blender, or transfer to a standard blender or food processor to puree.
5. Add olive oil to finish.
6. Season to taste with salt and pepper.
7. Divide into four bowls and garnish with Three Sisters Salsa (see below).

INGREDIENTS FOR THREE SISTERS SALSA

½ cup small-diced squash, seeded and skinned, and slightly roasted
½ cup corn kernels
½ cup green beans, blanched, and cut into ½ inch pieces
1½ teaspoons red pepper flakes
2 tablespoons olive oil
½ teaspoon minced cilantro
1 teaspoon lemon juice
Salt and pepper

PROCEDURE FOR THREE SISTERS SALSA

1. Mix all the ingredients together in a small bowl.

ASH ADAMS

OLIVE OIL POTATOES

MAKES 4 TO 6 SERVINGS

Holy moly, these are delicious! There is no shortage of potatoes in Alaska, whether we are talking about variety or quantity. The best time to try these is in the fall, before the first frost sets the tender skins. I love their velvety texture and rich finish.

Yukon Gold, Rose Finn, or any sweet, high-moisture, low-starch potato will work great. Get crazy and try the Magic Molly for a deep purple mash to get your Willy Wonka on. Rarely do I peel my potatoes—I enjoy the texture of the skins—but if you want to, go right ahead.

INGREDIENTS

1½ pounds Alaska Yukon Gold or Red Finn potatoes

1 cup olive oil

¾ cup grated Parmesan cheese

Salt and pepper

PROCEDURE

1. Rinse potatoes. I usually don't peel them, but for presentation purposes you can. Cut into equal-size pieces so they cook evenly.
2. Add potatoes into a pot and cover with water. Bring to a boil, drop to a simmer, and cook until fork tender, about 25 minutes.
3. Warm the olive oil in a small pan.
4. When the potatoes are tender, strain, place in a mixer with a paddle, or in a bowl and mash with a sturdy whisk.
5. Cautiously add the olive oil, incorporating by thirds, adding the Parmesan cheese in between rounds of oil.
6. When mixed thoroughly, add salt and pepper to taste.
7. If you are using a starchy potato such as a russet, you may need to add additional olive oil for a smooth, velvety consistency.

RED WINE BARLEY RISOTTO

MAKES 4 SERVINGS

The most important thing to remember when cooking with wine is to use a bottle you would indeed drink. This risotto holds up brilliantly to game and red meat. When finishing the risotto, it is very important to remove from the burner and emulsify (stir/mix in) the butter and cheese into the risotto. This keeps all that beautiful fat incorporated into the risotto, and not an oily mess oozing out everywhere.

INGREDIENTS

2 tablespoons olive oil
1 teaspoon minced garlic
1 yellow onion, diced small
2 stalks of celery, diced small
½ cup pearl barley
½ cup good red wine
1½ cups vegetable stock or water
4 tablespoons unsalted butter
2 tablespoons grated Parmesan cheese

PROCEDURE

1. In a thick-gauge medium-size pot, sweat garlic, onion, and celery.
2. When translucent, add barley and coat with olive oil. Add a little more oil if needed.
3. Add the red wine and stir frequently. When the wine is absorbed into the barley, add the stock.
4. Add roughly a third of the cooking liquid and stir frequently. When the liquid is absorbed, add another third.
5. When the barley has bloomed, or cooked to a point that the raw texture is gone when biting down on a grain of rice, spread it on a cookie pan and let cool, so it does not overcook.
6. Heat pan to medium, and pour in a half cup of vegetable stock.
7. When it starts to steam, add barley and desired veggies.
8. Remove from heat, and add butter and cheese.
9. Salt and pepper to taste.

ROASTED ROOT VEGGIES

MAKES 2 TO 4 SERVINGS

My wife and I have been making this for years, for a quick dinner or snack that can easily be reheated when returning home from a night of dinner service.

When we opened a diner, we put these on the menu, thinking that it would be to have something healthy for us to eat once in a while. We added them onto the sandwiches as an alternative to hand-cut fries. To our surprise, nearly half the sandwiches were ordered with roasted veggies. If you want to fancy it up, add a creole spice (see page 91) or Moroccan (see page 96) spice mix to them.

INGREDIENTS

1 beet, cut ½ inch by ½ inch by 3 inches

1 carrot, cut ½ inch by ½ inch by 3 inches

1 parsnip, cut ½ inch by ½ inch by 3 inches

¼ cup olive oil

Salt and pepper to taste

PROCEDURE

1. Preheat oven to 400°F. Cover a baking sheet with parchment paper.
2. Roll veggies in oil, and season with salt and pepper (or other spice mix)
3. Place veggies on a baking sheet and roast until cooked through, about 20 minutes.
4. If serving for dinner after they've cooled down, warm again in the oven for 5 to 7 minutes.
5. When cool enough to handle, stack on a plate to eat.

ASH ADAMS

ALASKA SALMON HEAD PHO

MAKES 4 SERVINGS

I wrote this recipe for renowned blogger and chef Emma Frisch, who hosted a blog feature called *A Bristol Bay Salmon Five Days, Five Ways*. I really wanted to include a recipe that utilized all portions of the fish.

This pho is based on a fish head soup. Traditionally, fish heads were cooked down long enough to leach calcium in an otherwise dairy-free culture. Adding a seaweed or beach green high in vitamins and minerals helps the omega-3s and vitamin D to be absorbed into the bloodstream. This process is a great natural balancing act that compensates for the lack of sunlight in the winter in Alaska. It further demonstrates the resilience and resourcefulness of Alaska's indigenous people.

INGREDIENTS FOR PHO

- 2 tablespoons vegetable oil
- 1 yellow onion, peeled and halved
- 3 garlic cloves, smashed
- 5 quarter-size slices fresh ginger
- 1 wild Alaska salmon head, gills removed, and rinsed in cold water
- 1 cinnamon stick
- 2 star anise
- 8 quarts water
- ½ teaspoon ground cinnamon
- ½ teaspoon ground star anise
- 3 tablespoons hoisin sauce
- 1 tablespoon Sriracha (optional)

PROCEDURE FOR PHO

1. Heat oil in a large pot over medium-high heat.
2. Add onion, garlic, and ginger. Cook while stirring constantly, 2 to 3 minutes.
3. Chop salmon head in half and add to pot along with the cinnamon stick, star anise, and water.
4. Let simmer 2 hours, adding more water as needed to keep head submerged while cooking.
5. Strain broth through a fine-mesh sieve, reserving head and discarding the rest.
6. Stir in ground cinnamon and ground star anise, hoisin, and Sriracha, if desired.
7. Return to a boil, then reduce heat and simmer 15 minutes. Set aside.

INGREDIENTS FOR NOODLES AND VEGETABLES

8 ounces rice vermicelli

½ onion, julienned

1 carrot, julienned

½ zucchini, julienned

½ Snow Apple or turnip or daikon radish, julienned

1 cup leafy greens, such as kale or chard, cut into ¼-inch ribbons

Fresh bean sprouts, basil leaves, torn cilantro for garnish, as desired

PROCEDURE FOR NOODLES AND VEGETABLES

1. Place rice noodles in a large bowl.
2. Boil enough water to cover noodles; pour over noodles.
3. Cover with plastic until noodles are soft and tender.
4. Drain noodles.
5. In a separate bowl add julienned onion, carrot, zucchini, turnip,and kale with 1 teaspoon of kosher salt.
6. Mix thoroughly and let sit for 7 minutes. When wilted, but still having some texture, add the noodles and mix well with garnish-sprouts and herbs.
7. Season to taste.

INGREDIENTS FOR PAN-SEARED SALMON FILLETS (optional)

4 Alaska salmon fillets, skinless and pin bones removed

Ground cinnamon, ground star anise, and salt, to taste

PROCEDURE FOR PAN-SEARED SALMON FILLETS

1. If topping pho with additional salmon pieces, dry salmon with a paper towel to remove excess moisture.
2. Season with cinnamon, ground star anise, and salt.
3. In a sauté pan over medium-high heat, add 1 tablespoon oil and place fish in pan.
4. Cook approximately 2 minutes, flip, and cook another 1 to 2 minutes until desired temperature; set aside.

PROCEDURE FOR PLATING

1. To serve pho, divide noodles evenly among four large bowls.
2. Top with vegetable strips, herbs, and pieces of cooked salmon—either the individual portions or meat from the head or the smoked salmon.
3. Pour broth over all.
4. Garnish with sprouts, basil leaves, and cilantro.

For six years I was affiliated with the Sitka Seafood Festival. The mission was to celebrate Alaska seafood, which is easy to do on Baranof Island, because Sitkans certainly like their celebrating!

For a week a year, my family would go to Sitka to coordinate a five-course seafood dinner with a guest chef or two from around the country and a phenomenal core group of dedicated residents to prep food, drink sponsored beer from Baranof Island Brewing Company, hang with some amazing friends and family (with more beer), gather local foods from local gardens and foragers, prepare the chowder for Saturday's festival, and parade (with more celebrating).

Quite frankly, this chowder has had many incarnations over the years. It's always had five criteria—seafood, pork product, potatoes, cream, and tardiness, due to its chef's lag time and the prior night's

2015 Sitka Seafood Festival Fish Tote Race with fellow chef partner Emma Frisch. Lifejacket and tutu—safety first. PHOTO COURTESY OF EMMA FRISCH.

View from Master Sitka Gardener Florence Welch. Mount Edgecumbe (dormant volcano) in the background. ROB KINNEEN

shenanigans. Over the years it became thoroughly Alaskafied, with more and more regional ingredients. The unsexy reality is that when you cut hundreds of pounds of whole fish and fillets, you will have a lot of chunks left over. In restaurants, where every dollar matters, we make sure to utilize everything, with as little waste as possible. This is a big recipe, so invite friends over and do some celebrating!

My grandfather, Noble Williams, passed away about 20 years ago. He was Tlingit, from the village of Sitka, a town of 9,500 people today, but it has been around for thousands of years. Totem Park is the original village site of the Tlingit people living there, and holds thousands of years of history. Walking around Totem Park, learning about local foods and traditions, exploring on boat rides and in the mountains has brought me closer to my Alaska heritage. It meant the world to me, showing my daughter and wife where our Tlingit people are from—the land, water, and trees.

2014 Sitka Seafood Festival guest chef Seth Caswell preparing for the Saturday parade. FISH ON!!
ROB KINNEEN

Sylvie and Dad getting our parade on.
ROB KINNEEN

SITKA SEAFOOD FESTIVAL CHOWDER

MAKES 12 SERVINGS

INGREDIENTS

½ cup vegetable oil

½ cup medium-diced reindeer sausage (recommended: Indian Valley Meats mild Polish reindeer sausage

1 cup medium-diced yellow onion

1 cup medium-diced celery

2 cloves garlic, minced

½ cup flour

2 cups beer (recommended: Baranof Island Brewing Company Silver Bay IPA or Redoubt Red)

1 quart fish stock, or prepared vegetable stock

2 cups medium-diced potatoes

1 cup warm cream

2 cups medium-chunked seafood (cod, halibut, salmon)

2 teaspoons Worcestershire sauce

1 teaspoon Tabasco

2 tablespoons unsalted butter

Salt

Pepper

Finishing salt (recommended: Alaska Pure Alder Smoked Flake Salt)

**You can substitute chorizo for reindeer sausage.*

PROCEDURE

1. In a 4-quart pot over medium heat, add ¼ cup oil and reindeer sausage. Cook until aromatic and browned, 3 to 4 minutes.
2. Add onion and celery, and cook until translucent, about 2 minutes, stirring occasionally.
3. Add garlic and cook until aromatic (30 to 45 seconds). Then add remaining ¼ cup oil and ½ cup flour. Using a small whisk, stir for 2 minutes to "cook out" the flour, which should look slightly tanned.
4. Add beer, and stir to incorporate with the flour. When it starts to thicken, add the fish stock and stir.
5. Add potatoes. Once the mix comes to a boil, drop to a slow simmer, on medium-low heat, and stir on occasion for 15 to 20 minutes.
6. If it starts sticking to the bottom, turn off and remove from the heat for 5 minutes. Anything sticking should lift from the bottom of the pan; check for scorching. If scorched, it is best to remove from pan.
7. After 20 minutes, the potatoes should be cooked through, and the whole soup should be thick enough to coat the back of a spoon.
8. Add the warmed cream and stir.
9. Fold in the fish and cook for 5 to 7 minutes to cook through.
10. Finish seasoning with Tabasco, Worcestershire sauce, salt, and pepper. I recommend Alaska Pure Smoked Alder Salt for some zip!

DANDELION PESTO POTATOES

MAKES 6 TO 8 SERVINGS

Oh, Alaska and potatoes . . .

I like to get nice fingerlings and cut them in half lengthwise.

Dandelions are more commonly known as pesky nuisances in manicured yards, but historically they were very popular foods for indigenous Alaskans. They are nutritionally beneficial, and this might be why they are so resilient as a plant.

Dandelion greens are very herbal with a tart finish. I find them very refreshing. Please do not rip them off a city sidewalk and cook with them! While foraging is all the rage, we need to remember to forage from safe and pesticide-free locations.

INGREDIENTS FOR POTATOES

2 pounds Alaska fingerling potatoes

½ cup vegetable oil

2 teaspoons kosher salt

PROCEDURE FOR POTATOES

1. Preheat oven to 350°F.
2. In a bowl, roll the cut potatoes in salt and oil.
3. Place on a baking sheet lined with parchment paper.
4. Roast until you can pierce easily with a knife, with a nice browned color, about 14 to 18 minutes.

INGREDIENTS FOR PESTO

2 cups dandelion greens (reserve one cup)

¼ cup cashew nuts

1 clove garlic

½ cup olive oil

PROCEDURE FOR PESTO

1. In a blender, combine dandelion greens, cashews, garlic and oil. Puree, then set side.

PROCEDURE FOR PLATING

1. Warm potatoes in a sauté pan.
2. When potatoes are warm through, add the pesto and the reserved one cup of dandelion greens.
3. Finish with salt and pepper to taste, and if needed, 2 ounces water to keep potatoes from sticking.

ROASTED GARLIC PUREE

MAKES ABOUT 2 CUPS

I worked for a spell at the now-closed Magnolia Grill in Durham, North Carolina. Ben and Karen Barker are pretty fantastic at caressing minutiae out of food, leading to huge flavors.

One of my favorite things at the Grill was the roasted garlic. We would take heads of garlic and slow roast them in liberal amounts of oil, and once they were cooked we would pass them through a food mill, discarding the skins and saving both the garlic puree and oil.

That oil can be used for marinades or added to vinaigrettes. The subtle-round flavor is deliciousness in a bottle.

When I returned home after a night of service, my wife would look up midconversation: "What were you eating?" I may or may not have snuck a spoonful or three of roasted garlic for personal consumption. I guess there can be too much of a good thing.

INGREDIENTS

4 cups vegetable oil

2 cups (or four heads*) of garlic

**If using whole heads, you must have a food mill on hand.*

PROCEDURE

1. Preheat oven to 350°F.
2. In a pie pan add the garlic and oil. Cover with foil.
3. Cook until done—about 45 minutes to one hour.
4. Let cool. If using garlic cloves, puree with a hand mixer. If using garlic heads, bust them up and pass through a food mill with the finest screen.
5. Reserve oil for marinades and vinaigrettes. Use the garlic puree for dressings, vinaigrettes, and various other goodness.

BAGNA CAUDA VINAIGRETTE

INGREDIENTS

¼ cup fresh lemon juice (add zest as well)

2 tablespoons Dijon mustard

1 teaspoon honey

1 teaspoon roasted garlic

1 cup olive oil

3 tablespoons water (if needed)

½ clove garlic, minced

3 white anchovies, chopped

2 teaspoons chopped fresh oregano

2 teaspoons chopped fresh parsley

2 teaspoons capers

½ teaspoon red pepper flake

Salt and pepper to taste

PROCEDURE

1. Add vinegar, mustard, honey, and garlic into a container together.
2. Using an immersion blender, slowly incorporate the oil to make an emulsion.
3. Add two tablespoons of water if you need to make the emulsion more viscous.
4. Fold in the remaining ingredients. It will provide a nice texture to the dressing.

For best results, make the dressing a day in advance to allow the flavors to mingle together.

TZATZIKI

This deliciousness sings from June to September, when local cucumbers come on the scene.

INGREDIENTS

½ red onion, julienne

½ English cucumber, cut into strips

½ teaspoon red pepper flakes

Zest and juice of 1 lemon

1 teaspoon kosher salt

2 teaspoons fresh mint

1 cup Greek yogurt

1 teaspoon roasted garlic oil

PROCEDURE

1. Mix all ingredients. Let sit at least 1 hour before serving.

Best before two days.

A WORD ON STOCKS

At home I like to save the shells from shrimp or crab to make a stock. After shelling, I wrap and store them in a storage bag in the freezer until there is enough to make a batch of stock.

I have seen kitchens that save carrot peels, the crummy outer layer of onions, red pepper seeds, and stems. I do not recommend doing this! Garbage in equals garbage out, and these stocks will be bitter and cloudy.

Sure, save the ends of carrots, onion pieces, and celery butts. But make sure they are clean and that there are appropriate ratios for the flavor of stock you're after. For additional flavor coat the vegetables or bones in oil, roast in the pan or in the oven to brown. For ease and versatility I made all the stocks omitting this step.

VEGETABLE STOCK

MAKES 2 QUARTS

INGREDIENTS

1½ pounds onions, rough chopped

¾ pound carrot, rough chopped

¾ pound celery, rough chopped

¼ cup garlic, rough chopped

Optional herbs (parsley, oregano, thyme)

2 quarts, 1 pint water

PROCEDURE

1. Bring all ingredients to a boil, then drop to a simmer.
2. Cook for 30 minutes, then strain.

CRAB AND SHRIMP STOCK

MAKES 3 QUARTS

When making a shellfish stock, bring water to a boil, drop to a simmer, and cook for no more than an hour. Strain the stock, and if you want to reduce the stock further, do so without the shells—this will keep the stock from becoming bitter.

INGREDIENTS

1 pound(ish) shrimp and/or crab shells

½ lb onion, rough chop

¼ lb celery, rough chop

3 ea garlic cloves, smashed

3 quarts water

PROCEDURE

1. Soak shells in ice water for 10 minutes to clean them before cooking. Rinse thoroughly.
2. In 3 quarts water, bring all ingredients up to a boil, drop to a simmer.
3. Cook for 45 minutes.
4. Strain and cool.
5. If not using in two days, portion and freeze.

FISH STOCK

MAKES 3 QUARTS

INGREDIENTS

3 pounds whitefish bones; If using fish heads, be sure to remove gills*

½ pound onion, rough chop

¼ pound celery, rough chop

3 garlic cloves, smashed

3 quarts water

**For best results, use non-oily white fish, such as rockfish or halibut bones.*

PROCEDURE

1. Soak the bones in ice water for 10 minutes to clean them before cooking.
2. In 3 quarts water, bring all ingredients up to a boil, then drop to a simmer.
3. Cook for 45 minutes.
4. Strain and cool.
5. If not using in two days, portion and freeze.

CHICKEN STOCK

MAKES ABOUT 2 QUARTS

This is where buying a whole chicken starts to pay dividends. Think hot and comforting chicken soup!

INGREDIENTS

¼ cup vegetable oil

1 onion, rough chopped

6 ribs celery, rough chopped

4 cloves of garlic, smashed

3 pounds chicken bones (two carcasses)

2 bay leaves

4 quarts water*

**2 cups dry white wine can be substituted for part of the water.*

PROCEDURE

1. In a stock pot over medium-high heat, add oil, onion, celery, and garlic, and cook until translucent. Turn the heat down if needed. Cook for 6 to 8 minutes.
2. Add the chicken bones, water, and bay leaves. If you are using wine, start with the wine and finish with water. Bring to a boil, then drop to a simmer.
3. Simmer for 2 hours. I like to have the heat off center so that the impurities (scum) that come off collect at the side of the pot with no heat, making for easy removal with a spoon or ladle.
4. When finished, strain and cool. Use in a day or two, or freeze.

BRIAN ADAMS

BRISTOL BAY

The pristine Bristol Bay region is famous for being home to the last prolific wild salmon run in the world. The salmon fishing season there lasts from mid-June to late July, but during this short time, 40 percent of the world's wild salmon is harvested commercially, and people visit from all over the world to enjoy excellent sportfishing.

Bristol Bay is located in the easternmost arm of the Bering Sea. A number of rivers flow into this bay, including the Cinder, Egegik, Igushik, Kvichak, Meshik, Nushagak, Naknek, Togiak, and Ugashik. The upper reaches of Bristol Bay experience some of the highest tides in the world. Even on a good day, the weather can change on a dime, tides swell, clouds cover the mountains, and rain arrives in sheets. This rugged, temperamental, beautiful land is one of many in Alaska accessible only by boat or plane.

My eyes were opened to the plight of the salmon while listening to David Montgomery, author of *The King of Fish*, speak at a panel in Sitka. The following year I had the good fortune of meeting Mark Titus, producer and director of the documentary film *The Breach*. Learning from these two and speaking with the residents there, it is crystal clear that we desperately need to protect and preserve the special place that is Bristol Bay.

For a host of reasons, salmon have been reduced to a fraction of their former populations in Europe, the British Isles, Canada, the eastern

Hand-crafted hot-smoked salmon strips. BRIAN ADAMS

United States, and the West Coast—everywhere but Alaska. While indigenous Alaskans have lived on wild salmon for thousands of years, the first commercial cannery here opened in the late 1800s, in Bristol Bay. Until the 1950s, Bristol Bay boats were powered by sail! To this day, by law, boats are still only thirty-two feet long, although their width has grown substantially. This allows them to navigate in the rough and narrow channels.

On a media tour in 2015, I was able to experience Bristol Bay's beauty firsthand. Experiences I will always remember include sport-fishing on the Naknek River, and even actually catching a king salmon! I also stayed at the stunning Bear Trail Lodge and met the owner and one of the first ladies of sportfishing, Nancy Lyons. Nancy also runs an educational program to train local youth in the hospitality and sportfishing industries.

Meeting the state employees who monitor and estimate the return time of the salmon population on an annual basis, in order to uphold the Alaska state constitution, was inspiring. Bristol Bay commercial fishery is strictly managed to ensure that a set amount of salmon returning from their five-year journey are allowed access upstream to spawn.

Despite past hardships and local competition, the businesses and people of Bristol Bay have come together to protect the salmon—in essence preserving this unique and amazing way of life.

Bristol Bay fishing boats prepare to fish on a foggy morning. BRIAN ADAMS

This is a container of red salmon caught by subsistence permit on the beaches of king salmon. Subsistence fishing is very important to families around the state and it becomes more important the more remote you go, as food and fuel prices rise. BRIAN ADAMS

BRIAN ADAMS

SEAFOOD

When I think of seafood in Alaska, salmon, king crab, and halibut immediately come to mind. And for those living in Alaska, the list continues: rockfish, Dungeness and snow crab, spot shrimp, razor clams, scallops, cod, black cod, regional fish like sheefish on the Kobuk River, herring, smelt, and countless others, whether you want to ice fish, dip net, or long line as a resident of the state.

Alaska has 33,000 miles of coastline—more than the rest of the US combined—and one million square miles of fishing waters around the state. We have Bristol Bay, home to the world's largest fishing reserve and largest wild salmon run in the world.

There have been great strides to recapture salmon runs as well. Tyonek, a little village at the base of Sleeping Lady (Mount Susitna) on the banks of Cook Inlet, has raised money to restore salmon runs with large culverts that allow salmon access to traditional runs. These have been successful efforts.

Alaska is the only state in the nation with sustainable fisheries written into its constitution. One aspect of this kind of sustainability-in-action

Adem's custom-made wagon, working hard. BRIAN ADAMS

is a program offered to grow industry in rural western Alaska in the Bering Sea and Aleutian regions. This Community Development Quota Program provides support for eligible communities to participate and invest in fisheries programs in their area, creating sustainable and diversified economies.

A great example of this is the Norton Sound Economic Development Corporation (NSEDC), located in Nome on the Seward Peninsula.

Originally from Anchorage, Adem Boekmann has happily relocated to Nome. With the help of the NSEDC, he captains a crab boat during the ice-free season, and also ice crabs in the winter for a select time. Driving his snow machine with a customized sled, he checks his thirty crab pots on the frozen Norton Sound during late March and early April. The king crab he catches is sent live all around the world.

Seafood is a force in Alaska on an economic, community, nourishment, traditional, and spiritual level. Upholding the state's constitution and taking care of Alaska's beautiful resource is vital.

En route via snow machine to one of the thirty pots laid out in the Norton Sound. BRIAN ADAMS

Norton Sound king crab. BRIAN ADAMS

ARCTIC SHRIMP AND GRITS WITH BACON AND RED-EYE GRAVY

MAKES 2 ENTRÉES OR 4 APPETIZERS

Alaska ingredients, together with the time I spent in the South, inspired this recipe. Generally speaking, ingredients in traditional recipes have way more to do with ease of availability and versatility. Shrimp and grits is a coastal Southern American Gullah dish. Red-eye gravy, from what I've found, is thrifty breakfast cooking adapted for a greasy-spoon truck-stop diner: country ham or bacon cooked in a pan and deglazed with coffee. The coffee forms the pupil, and the fat from the cooked pork is the rest of the eye surrounding it. Onward and upward...I love getting my fancy on with humble, true ingredients.

I am a spice wimp, and this sauce is a little punchy. It should mellow out with the addition of the grits, but if you find yourself averse to heat, I would turn down the Tabasco.

Serve over Arctic Grits (recipe page 36).

INGREDIENTS

- 1 teaspoon vegetable oil
- ⅓ cup small-diced bacon or pancetta
- ½ cup small-diced red onion
- ¼ cup small-diced celery
- ¼ cup small-diced red pepper
- 1 teaspoon minced garlic
- 12 spot shrimp (21/25 size, if available)
- 2 teaspoons Bamnation Creole Spice (see page 91)
- 2 cups brewed coffee
- 1 teaspoon Tabasco
- 2 tablespoons Worcestershire
- 2 tablespoons butter

PROCEDURE

1. In a pan over medium heat, add the oil and diced bacon.
2. When rendered out, add the onion, celery, and peppers (also known as the Cajun holy trinity).
3. As the trinity is becoming translucent, add the garlic and shrimp, after rolling it in the Creole Spice.
4. Flip the shrimp, add the coffee, then simmer to reduce by half.
5. Add Tabasco and Worcestershire.
6. Finish with butter.
7. As the shrimp are cooked (just a minute or two per side), remove from pan.
8. Fold in butter at the end.
9. Three shrimp per plate, or six per entrée. Cover with veggies and sauce over the grits.

BRIAN ADAMS

ASH ADAMS

BRAISED ROCKFISH WITH FUMET, VEGETABLES, SEAWEED, AND SEAL OIL

MAKES 4 SERVINGS

Around 2010, I was becoming a little disillusioned with Alaska's food culture. Learning that 96 percent of our food was being imported into the state did not help. The increased awareness of value-added foods and movements away from handcrafting drove me in another direction.

This recipe is from a video web series I did in collaboration with Alaska Native Tribal Health Consortium called *Traditional Foods, Contemporary Chef.* I am Tlingit-Southeast Alaska Native. Southeast Alaska Native ingredients, massaged with a contemporary recipe spin, inspired this recipe.

Obviously, there are a few items that are not easy to come by if you don't live in Southeast Alaska. I would consider taking creative liberties in this case. Use a local white fish that can stand up to being pan-seared. Alter the seaweed with either a wakame salad or a local herb that can hold up to cooking. Last, substitute for seal oil with a flavored olive oil or reduction that will complement the dish. My inspiration was drizzling a fine olive oil over seafood, like you would with Mediterranean-inspired cooking.

INGREDIENTS FOR SEAFOOD FUMET

4 pounds fish bones rinsed in ice water until the water runs clear, also remove gill plate if cooking head

½ onion, rough chopped

3 celery stalks, rough chopped

3 cloves of garlic, smashed

12 cups water

½ lemon, reserve to finish

PROCEDURE FOR SEAFOOD FUMET

1. Combine all ingredients in a stock pot. Bring to a boil, drop to a simmer, and cook for 45 minutes.
2. Finish with a fresh squeeze of lemon juice.
3. Strain, and reserve liquid.
4. It is common to process fish for the broth and to make more than needed for a specific recipe. Freeze unused portions for future use.

INGREDIENTS FOR BRAISING LIQUID

3 tablespoons olive oil
½ cup small-diced onion
½ cup small-diced celery
½ teaspoon red pepper flakes
1 clove of garlic, minced
¾ cup small-diced potatoes
8 cups fumet

PROCEDURE FOR BRAISING LIQUID

1. In a saucepan over medium heat, sweat onions and celery.
2. When translucent, add garlic and potatoes, and stir to keep from sticking.
3. Add stock and bring to a boil. Drop to simmer for 12 to 15 minutes, or until the potatoes are tender.

INGREDIENTS FOR PLATING

3 tablespoons olive oil
4 6-ounce portions of rockfish
2 cups fumet with cooked vegetables
1 cup fumet, reserve if additional broth is needed
4 tablespoons yarrow or other green
2 tablespoons wild parsley or other green
4 tablespoons seaweed (dried black or kombu) or wakame salad if available
4 tablespoons seal oil or extra virgin olive oil for garnish

PROCEDURE FOR PLATING

1. In a sauté pan over medium heat, add oil and then sear rockfish skin side down.
2. Press down lightly with spatula to make sure skin sears well.
3. When you notice a hard white line, flip in pan.
4. Add fumet with vegetables, bring to a boil, drop to a simmer, and let cook for 8 to 10 minutes, depending on thickness of fish.
5. Finish with seaweed and foraged greens, just wilted.
6. Plate with fish on bottom, broth and veggies over the top, and seal oil drizzled over the plate.

AN ADAMS

ASH AD

BRISTOL BAY SALMON OVER FORAGED RICE PASTA AND TUNDRA VINAIGRETTE

MAKES 4 SERVINGS

On a media tour in 2015, I had the chance to see the Bristol Bay fisheries firsthand. The fishery season only lasts six to eight weeks, yet it yields 50 percent of the wild salmon market globally, equating to twenty-eight million pounds of wild Alaska salmon!

Despite the massive business, the Bristol Bay region is very remote and only accessible by boat or plane. Traditional and subsistence foods are very important to this community. This recipe was meant to honor both sides of this world: the worldwide importance of wild Bristol Bay salmon, as well as the unique flavors of the rocky and temperamental coast and the aromatic, marshy tundra.

INGREDIENTS FOR SALMON

4 6-ounce portions Bristol Bay salmon, skin off and pin boned

2 tablespoons vegetable oil

Kosher salt and pepper to taste

PROCEDURE FOR SALMON

1. For best results, pull salmon out of refrigerator 5 minutes before cooking.
2. Before putting salmon in pan, dab it with a paper towel, whisking away residual moisture, and season with salt and pepper.
3. In a sauté pan over medium-high heat, add oil.
4. Add salmon to the pan flesh side down, and be sure to release away from you, so as not to splash oil in your direction. Do not crowd the fish.
5. Pick up after 1 minute, to avoid sticking.
6. Gently flip salmon, and depending on the thickness, turn the heat off and let it rest in the pan as you plate the rest of the meal.

INGREDIENTS FOR FORAGED PASTA

2 cups cooked rice noodles

2 tablespoons vegetable oil

1 cup beach greens or other hearty green

½ cup beach peas or domestic sweet peas

1 cup mustard greens, chiffonade, or domestic greens

Beach pea tendrils (as garnish) or locally purchased

Beach pea blossoms (as garnish) or microgreens

Kosher salt and pepper to taste

This is a very region-specific recipe—for best results, speak with a local forager in your community or visit your local farmers market. Be sure you harvest these items from a reliable person.

PROCEDURE FOR FORAGED PASTA

1. Be sure to wash all foraged items in a diluted vinegar wash.
2. Heat the oil in a sauté pan over medium-high heat.
3. Add the beach peas, and cook for 45 seconds. Add beach greens and mustard greens.
4. After 45 seconds, or when the greens begin to wilt, turn off heat and add noodles, stirring constantly.
6. If needed, add a tablespoon or two of water to steam and lift items off the bottom of the pan.
7. Add approximately ¼ cup of the dressing to the noodle mixture and carefully mix in.
8. Divide and plate on warmed plates.

INGREDIENTS FOR TUNDRA VINAIGRETTE

½ cup apple cider vinegar

1 teaspoon Dijon mustard

1 teaspoon roasted garlic

1 tablespoon honey

½ cup vegetable oil

2 tablespoons Labrador tea, dried and broken up*

2 tablespoons wormwood (stinkweed), dried and broken up

**Please recognize that Labrador tea and wormwood are used as both food and medicine historically. Please practice moderation when consuming.*

PROCEDURE FOR TUNDRA VINAIGRETTE

1. Add vinegar, mustard, and garlic together into a container.
2. Strongly mix in the oil to make an emulsion.
3. Add 2 tablespoons of water if you need to make the emulsion more viscous.
4. Add wormwood and Labrador tea at the end.

For best results, make the dressing a day in advance to allow the flavors to mingle together.

BRIAN ADAMS

CLAMS AND SAUSAGE IN A WHITE WINE BROTH

MAKES 2 ENTRÉES OR 4 APPETIZERS

This is an Alaska take on a very traditional Italian dish. I worked for an Italian trattoria in Durham, North Carolina, and over time, I was swept into the beautiful simplicity of Italian food. Seemingly simple fare was based on quality ingredients with minimal execution.

INGREDIENTS

2 tablespoons vegetable oil

1 pound Alaska razor clams, cleaned and chopped, juice reserved

1 8-ounce reindeer sausage,* quartered lengthwise, sliced into ½-inch pieces, and roasted in the oven for 12 minutes (recommended: Indian Valley Meats mild Polish reindeer sausage)

¼ teaspoon red pepper flakes

1 clove garlic, sliced

½ cup white wine

¾ cup vegetable stock

2 tablespoons butter

½ pound linguine, cooked

Salt and pepper to taste

2 tablespoons chopped parsley

**If reindeer sausage isn't available, choose a different type of sausage such as chorizo or Italian sausage.*

PROCEDURE

1. Heat the oil in a sauté pan over medium heat. Add clams, garlic, and red pepper flakes.
2. Stir frequently to ensure that the oil coats all the clams and that they are cooking evenly.
3. When the garlic is soft and releases its fragrance, deglaze by adding the wine.
4. Continue cooking until wine reduces by half.
5. Add the stock, and continue to simmer for 1 minute.
6. Add the linguine and parsley, and season with salt and pepper to taste.
7. Divide into four small serving bowls if serving as a starter, or two larger bowls for entrées.

ASH ADAMS

HOUSE-MADE SALT COD OVER OLIVE OIL POTATOES

MAKES 4 ENTRÉES OR 8 APPETIZERS

Salt cod is a traditional preparation used to provide dry protein for Spanish explorers. The only way to really eat it is to rehydrate it in milk or water for two days or to mix it with potatoes or in a soup..

During some time in New York I ran across this method of quick-curing the cod. I love the rich, flaky texture it gives the fish. Be sure to use nonreactive (stainless steel) racks when drying the fish.

INGREDIENTS

4 pounds fillet of cod (Pacific cod or sablefish) portioned into 8-ounce pieces

½ cup kosher salt

4 cups water

1 quart ice

PROCEDURE

1. Combine 2 cups of water with ¼ cup salt and bring to a boil.
2. Put the ice in a pot, then cover with the salted water. Add the remaining water.
3. Place the fillets in the cool water for 10 minutes, making sure there is enough room for them to move around.
4. Remove the fillets and place on plastic risers, or nonreactive perforated pans.
5. Leave uncovered for three days, turning over every day. This will give a firm, dry exterior, referred to as a pellicle.
6. Serve with Olive Oil Potatoes (see page 41) and Bagna Cauda Vinaigrette (see page 51).

PAN-SEARED ALASKA HALIBUT CHEEKS IN A BIRCH-BROWN BUTTER SAUCE, SERVED OVER ALASKA HARVEST VEGETABLE TANGLE

MAKES 2 ENTRÉES OR 4 APPETIZERS

Growing up, it was common to see people in the know taking five-gallon buckets of halibut heads home to carve out the cheeks and freeze or eat them. The secret is officially out! As seafood prices rise, once-humble parts are being more regularly utilized. I love the texture of halibut cheeks, as the muscle structure is long and lean, different from the rest of the halibut flesh, and yet the cheeks remain oh so tender.

INGREDIENTS

2 tablespoons vegetable oil

8 ounces halibut cheeks, free of connective tissue

Salt and pepper to taste

4 tablespoons butter

2 tablespoons birch syrup

½ zucchini, julienne

1 turnip, julienne

¼ stalk rhubarb, julienne

4 kale leaves, julienne

1 tablespoon chopped mint

1 teaspoon red pepper flake

1 teaspoon kosher salt

PROCEDURE

1. Julienne zucchini into long strips. For best results discard seeds.
2. Repeat with turnip and rhubarb.
3. Salt with kosher salt, and let sit for 5 to 10 minutes.
4. Add in red pepper flakes and mint.

To sear the cheeks:

1. Pull halibut cheeks out of fridge about 5 to 10 minutes before using.
2. Using a dry cloth, remove any excess moisture from the halibut cheeks.
3. Heat oil in a pan over medium heat.
4. Place the cheeks in the oil gently, so they don't splash oil.
5. Cook for 1 to 1½ minutes. Make sure they are not sticking to the pan. Look for the transition of color on the cheeks from a translucent to a bright white.
6. Flip, let cook for 45 seconds, add butter and swirl, coating everything and gently turning the butter into a dark color with a nutty aroma. Remove from heat if necessary.
7. Add birch syrup and keep swirling.
8. Plate the tangle of vegetables and top with fish and sauce.

PAN-SEARED SCALLOPS WITH RAS EL HANOUT AND ROSE HIP VINAIGRETTE

MAKES 4 SERVINGS

Playing with the naturally sweet scallop and the tart rose hip vinaigrette is a fun and delicious treat!

INGREDIENTS FOR SCALLOPS

1⅓ pounds Alaska scallops (size U10 or U10–20)

¼ cup cooking oil

4 teaspoons Ras El Hanout Moroccan Spice (see recipe page 77)

½ cup Alaska Rose Hip Vinaigrette (see recipe below)

Salt to taste

PROCEDURE FOR SCALLOPS

1. For best results, place the scallops on a paper towel and dab the top of the scallops to remove excess moisture.
2. Let them sit at room temperature for 5 to 7 minutes and remove abductor muscle.
3. Roll the scallops liberally in the seasoning and a bit of salt.
4. In a sauté pan over medium-high heat, arrange the scallops.
5. Make sure not to crowd the pan, as it will cool down as you add the scallops.
6. Be certain that they are searing and not burning. After 30 to 45 seconds, scoot them around and check. The color of the flesh changes on the side closest to the pan. It should be translucent about a third of the way up the scallop before flipping them.
7. Take the pan off the heat and let the scallops rest in the pan until the desired temperature is achieved, usually medium-rare to medium.

ALASKA ROSE HIP VINAIGRETTE

I have always made it my business to work with local ingredients. This vinaigrette was something I found at a tourist shop and decided to try and work with.

This is naturally tart from the rose hips, which is why it plays so well with the sweet and delicate scallops.

INGREDIENTS

2 teabags Alaska Wild Teas Wild Rose tea

¼ cup hot water

¼ cup red wine vinegar

1 tablespoon Alaska Pure Fireweed Honey

½ teaspoon roasted garlic

1 teaspoon dry mustard

1 cup vegetable oil

Salt and pepper to taste

PROCEDURE

1. Steep the tea in hot water for 3 minutes. I like to actually tear open the bags, as the loose tea adds a lot of color and texture to the vinaigrette.
2. In a separate container, add vinegar, honey, roast garlic, dry mustard, and the steeped tea when it is tepid.
3. Blend well with an immersion blender, incorporating the oil to emulsify.
4. Season with salt and pepper to taste.

RAS EL HANOUT SPICE BLEND

Ras el hanout is a North African (Moroccan) spice blend. The specific ingredients are kind of loose, as the spices are market-driven. Some really neat periphery spices are grains of paradise and dried rosebuds, and both would be great additions to this blend.

INGREDIENTS

1 tablespoon ground cumin

1 tablespoon ground ginger

1 tablespoon turmeric

1 tablespoon salt

¾ tablespoon cinnamon

¾ tablespoon black pepper

½ tablespoon white pepper

½ tablespoon coriander

½ tablespoon cayenne

½ tablespoon allspice

½ tablespoon ground cloves

PROCEDURE

1. Mix all spices together. Super simple!

SALMON WITH PICKLED BEET VINAIGRETTE AND TOASTED QUINOA-ROOT VEGETABLE HASH

MAKES 4 SERVINGS

In 2010 I was awarded a grant from the State of Alaska Division of Agriculture to highlight winter root harvest crops in Alaska. The result was a three-part web series called *Fresh Alaska*, which included conversations with my favorite farmers, the VanderWeeles of VanderWeele Farms and Alex Davis of A.D. Farm. This was an effort to show people there were fresh Alaska alternatives and local produce, even in the cold winter months.

In Alaska's Matanuska Valley, seeding starts in April, with planting no earlier than May, when the fields are free of snow. By late June and early July, there are up to eighteen hours of daylight. During September, the weather cools, with declining daylight and possible freezing. October brings the first snows and freezing weather, and by November, fields are cleaned and the root harvest is secured in a dark, cool, dirty place. A farmer tries to fit a year's worth of work into six months.

The VanderWeeles grow a lot of volume, with three warehouses each the size of a high school gymnasium. They are able to sell carrots and potatoes all winter long to schools and local stores. Alex Davis, of A.D. Farm, started growing larger amounts of root harvest crops to keep selling year-round. Since 2011, his Center Market has operated once a week throughout the year, where he sells his naturally raised pork, farm-fresh eggs, and root harvest crops. This market grows every year with further additions of artisan vendors.

INGREDIENTS FOR SALMON

4 6-ounce portions of winter king salmon, skin off and pin boned

2 tablespoons vegetable oil

Kosher salt

Pepper

PROCEDURE FOR SALMON

1. For best results, pull salmon out of refrigerator 5 minutes before cooking.
2. Before putting salmon in pan, dab with a paper towel, whisking away residual moisture, and then season with salt and pepper.
3. In a sauté pan over medium-high heat, add oil.
4. Add salmon to the pan flesh side down, and be sure to it release away from you, so as not to splash oil in your direction. Do not crowd the fish.
5. Depending on the thickness of the salmon, it should take just a couple of minutes to cook.
6. Shift after a minute, to avoid sticking.
7. Gently flip salmon, with timing dependent on thickness.
8. Turn off heat and let rest in pan as you plate the rest of the meal.

INGREDIENTS FOR PICKLED BEETS

½ cup honey

4 cups water

1 teaspoon cloves

¼ stick cinnamon

6 peppercorns

2 cups red wine vinegar

2 pounds beets, top and bottom cut off

PROCEDURE FOR PICKLED BEETS

1. Preheat oven to 350°F.
2. Whisk together honey and water. Pour into an ovenproof pan with cinnamon, cloves, peppercorn, and vinegar.
3. When adding beets, make sure the tops and bottoms are cut off. Cut beets to the same size, to ensure equal cooking times.
4. Cover the beets with foil and bake until fork-tender. If necessary, add additional water and continue baking.
5. When beets are cooled off enough to handle, rub with a towel to remove skins.
6. Strain braising liquid over the peeled beets.
7. Keep in a refrigerator for up to a week.

INGREDIENTS FOR PICKLED BEET VINAIGRETTE

½ cup pickled beets, diced small (set aside ¼ cup for garnish)

1 teaspoon dry mustard

½ teaspoon garlic

4 tablespoons red wine vinegar

¾ cup vegetable oil

½ teaspoon thyme

½ teaspoon oregano

PROCEDURE FOR PICKLED BEET VINAIGRETTE

1. In a container add pickled beets, dry mustard, garlic, and red wine vinegar.
2. With an immersion blender, blend all ingredients thoroughly.
3. When mixed well, begin incorporating oil in a small drizzle.
4. You will hear a thickening sound; if the dressing gets too thick, add a little water to loosen viscosity. This makes the dressing more pleasant to eat and it keeps the emulsion from breaking
5. It is useful to have 1 ounce water on reserve to thin out vinaigrette to desired consistency.

INGREDIENTS FOR TOASTED QUINOA-ROOT VEGETABLE HASH

½ cup quinoa

1 cup water

½ cup medium-dice parsnips

½ cup medium-dice carrots

PROCEDURE FOR TOASTED QUINOA-ROOT VEGETABLE HASH

1. Preheat oven to 425°F.
2. Spread quinoa on a ridged pan lined with parchment paper. Toast quinoa for 5 to 7 minutes. Be sure to shake the pan so it doesn't get too dark. A peanut aroma will emerge when you are getting close.
3. Heat 1 cup of water in a large pot to a boil. Add the quinoa and watch for it to bubble and spit when the grain is added, especially if it is still warm from the oven.
4. Reduce to simmer and let cook for 12 minutes.
5. Turn off the heat and let steam for another 5 minutes.
6. On a ridged pan with parchment paper, spread out diced carrots and parsnips.
7. Bake for 10 minutes.
8. When finished, incorporate into the quinoa, and season with salt and pepper.

PROCEDURE FOR PLATING

1. Place a healthy scoop of the hash into the middle of a plate.
2. Position salmon on top of the hash.
3. Drizzle sauce over top of fish, and around well of plate.
4. Garnish with small diced pickled beets, and micro beet greens if available.

SEARED ROCKFISH OVER SHRIMP AND FORAGED FRIED RICE

MAKES 2 ENTRÉES OR 4 APPETIZERS

I've used this recipe many times to show how to cook simply with limited ingredients. It is hard to imagine even for me—a mostly lifelong Alaskan who's spent time in rural areas—that there are still areas of Alaska with no running water or indoor plumbing. Heating fuel is so expensive that many rural home cooks use an electric hot top rather than their stoves to prepare meals. Inexpensive ingredients like dried beans are not used, as they will take hours to cook!

When I've done cooking demonstrations in communities, I've tried to honor what is available—mostly food procured by local families like game meat, fish, and a variety of botanicals. It isn't beneficial to anyone for me to show up with fancy ingredients, cookware, or gadgets if they cannot be used or obtained. Sometimes the closest store is in the next town over . . . and you can only get there by plane!

This dish has been modified to include porcupine, duck, seafood, seal—wherever the plane takes me! A bag of rice and pantry staples like onions and carrots can almost always be found—if not fresh, then frozen or canned.

INGREDIENTS

2 tablespoons oil

½ carrot, diced small

½ daikon or turnip, diced small

½ yellow onion, diced small

1 teaspoon minced garlic

1 teaspoon minced ginger

2 cups cooked brown rice

6 ounces spot shrimp, cleaned and cut small

2 eggs, beaten

2 tablespoons soy sauce (use tamari for a gluten-free option)

1 cup beach greens, beach asparagus, or store-bought greens

1 cup bladderwrack seaweed, sliced thin, or rehydrated hijiki seaweed

2 tablespoons cooking oil

Salt and pepper

2 6-ounce skin-on rockfish fillets (or other white fish)

PROCEDURE FOR FORAGED RICE

1. Heat oil in a sauté pan over medium heat.
2. Sauté the onion, carrots, and daikon.
3. When the onion is translucent, add the garlic and ginger, stirring until fragrant.
4. Add rice and stir.
5. Make a well in the middle of the pan, add in the eggs, and scramble for 30 seconds.
6. Add the greens and shrimp, then deglaze with soy sauce.
7. Season to taste with salt and pepper.

PROCEDURE FOR ROCKFISH

1. Scale, debone, and score the rockfish skin—use your knife to make an X that pierces the skin to the white part of the flesh.
2. Keep the fish on a dry towel, skin side down, until you are ready to cook.
3. Season with salt and pepper just before laying the fish in the pan.
4. Over medium-high heat, add oil and lay the fish skin side down in the pan.
5. Keep the fish still, pressing with a spatula on occasion to make sure the fish does not buckle.
6. When the flesh changes from translucent to white, make sure the fish can move in the pan, flip, and let it rest to complete cooking.
7. This process should result in a crispy skin and tender-cooked flesh.

PROCEDURE FOR PLATING

1. Divide the rice into two entrée or four appetizer portions.
2. Top with a piece of the rockfish: 6 ounces if entrée, 3 ounces if appetizer.

INDIGENIZED CUISINE

BRIAN ADAMS

As a chef I have been using fresh foods from local producers and farmers markets for many years. Integrating indigenous Alaskan foods into my brush set proved a little challenging. Some foods translate easily: salmon, halibut, and crab. Some are found in homes from north to south, but you wouldn't or couldn't find them in restaurants: deer or moose, for example. Others could be considered taboo outside of Alaska Native culture: whale, seal, and walrus. Several foods are more widely available, and over the years are seen on more local menus: seaweed, berries, and botanicals (including spruce tips, fireweed tendrils, and fiddleheads).

I have had the good fortune to work with whale in Barrow, go ice crabbing and visit a reindeer ranch in Nome, prepare and serve that same reindeer in Washington, DC, cook porcupine and fish in Iliamna, work for six years as part of a multicourse seafood dinner program in Sitka, serve crab sushi in Kodiak, and forage for botanicals in Ketchikan, Hoonah, Juneau, Anchorage, Whittier, Kenai, Seward, Fairbanks, Bethel, and beyond. I have been on a seal and whale hunt in the Bering Sea, and cooked sheefish and salmon in Unalakleet and Kotzebue.

Quite a few of these experiences were parts of cooking demonstrations for diabetes prevention programs; I like to educate with entertainment. Discussing the nutritious benefits of eating indigenous foods and holding onto those traditions means making food work for people's everyday lives, while also engaging their environments—this can be very powerful.

Two events sparked my intense interest in Alaska indigenous cuisine.

Becoming a parent in 2010 led me to start thinking about indigenous food and what it meant. Through a series of collaborations, I have been able to connect with Alaska on a more intimate level.

The community of Flat Island pulling together to dress the harvest from the Bering Sea. ROB KINNEEN

Palm trees made of whale baleen and driftwood near Barrow at a traditional fish camp. This was taken in January, 2012, sightseeing at –40°F!!! ROB KINNEEN

As a parent, I don't want to give my daughter everything, but I want to prepare her for anything. This starts with knowing her story—who she is, and where she comes from. This made me aware of my own insecurities and questions about my heritage. My self-confidence grew in the kitchen. By integrating my stories of food and traditions, this carried me toward my current path.

Things had already begun percolating in my mind a year earlier. In 2009, I catered the *For the Rights of All* film premiere at the Smithsonian Institution's National Museum of the American Indian (NMAI) in Washington, DC. The documentary film discusses the Alaska civil rights movement, which occurred twenty years before similar national movements.

While cooking at NMAI, I also came across an exhibit called "Ramp It Up: Skateboard Culture in Native America." Through this traveling exhibition, the Wounded Knee Skateboards and Propaganda company has promoted Native American history to youth using the contemporary platform of skateboarding. Their mission instilled pride and knowledge of history within young people, focusing on powwows and reservations while also promoting health and athletics.

These powerful examples drove me to use my platform of food and culture to create a multilayered dialogue about indigenized foods:

Respecting traditional foods. Much like language, if a food culture is not used it will be forgotten. This means honoring the nutritional value of the food and understanding how it kept us healthy for thousands of years. Additionally, updating cooking techniques to accommodate a palate that may not have grown up on them—much like my own.

Creating a value for these foods. By using them in contemporary recipes, we may be looking at them in a new light. Value also means monetary. Traditionally, a subsistence lifestyle was common. There are

On the Bering Sea in a twenty-foot skiff, on the hunt with surprisingly traditional tools. ROB KINNEEN

still many people who straddle subsistence lifestyles in a cash-economy world. Foraging and cultivating traditional foods can create economies in rural areas.

Taking a moment to "overview" what we eat and why. A nutritionist working in rural Alaska might spit at the mere mention of pilot bread crackers or fry bread. The reality is these are commodity foods that have woven their way into the diet of Alaskans. What can we do to minimize the effects, or to treat them as they were meant to be, as an occasional snack? Or to put something healthy on top?

I started crafting my own take on indigenous cuisine. For example, while cooking for Al Roker of *The Today Show* when he visited Alaska in 2011, my menu offered spot shrimp fresh rolls with fireweed shoots and elk skewers, marinated in spruce tips with blueberry gastrique. While these dishes stand as some familiar multicultural forms, they were also my attempt to "indigenize" a menu with local Alaska flavor.

Later that summer, while executing a five-hundred-person banquet for the National Indian Health Board and attendees who were leaders of First Nations health organizations from all over the world, the menu was steeped in Alaska Native culture. Salmon, moose, whale, berries, herring eggs, and the summer bounty from foraged and local markets were on display at stations featuring food from different regions around Alaska.

And then that fall, boundaries were blurred further at the first Howard Rock and Ted Stevens Smokehouse Gala, a five-course high-end dinner and fundraiser for the First Alaskans Institute. I sported a "Tlingit bling" chef's jacket made to celebrate the event. This jacket featured traditional Tlingit artwork highlighting the Eagle clan from Southeast Alaska. Other attendees wore tuxedos with seal-fur-lined lapels, modified kuspuks, ball gowns featuring traditional beading and skins, and many other fashions that highlighted their regions.

The food was, again, a provocative glimpse into Alaska culture. Sailor Boy (hardtack cracker) croutons on a salad, reindeer sausage

On a hunt in the Bering Sea, October 2011. ROB KINNEEN

My "Tlingit bling" chef's jacket for the third annual Howard Rock and Ted Stevens Smokehouse Gala featuring an indigenized menu. ROB KINNEEN

and king crab Oscar (a riff on a decadent French dish), a seafood cocktail featuring local vodka in the sauce, and herring roe and spot shrimp with seaweed. Salmon and local beef graced the main course with farm-fresh veggies and botanicals sprinkled on the dish. Dessert: coffee-chocolate truffles, alder-smoked sea salt, and agudak.

One highlight of my culinary life was being handpicked to cook an indigenized multicourse dinner for President Barack Obama. In 2015, President Obama spent three days visiting Alaska to witness the effects of climate change firsthand. My team and I fed him in Anchorage, but his trip also took him to smaller Alaska villages, where he engaged with children, Elders, and the community. Later I saw footage of him dancing traditional dances at community events, bowled over by children and laughing overwhelmingly. He spoke to the crowd, encouraging them to be proud of their language, dance, and heritage, and telling them to carry it with them as they go into the world. I want to take the space here to thank him for those positive sentiments. Culture is not stagnant. It is evolving, and it should be embraced—it is not shameful, and not a burden.

Filming *Traditional Foods, Contemporary Chef* with the Alaska Native Tribal Health Consortium, our crew visited Stebbins and Alukanuk, two small villages on the coast of the Bering Sea. We were there to engage in a food intervention. Though we went to help, that week I walked away the richer person. We always learned many lessons on those trips, and witnessing communities that were still very much living a subsistence lifestyle was really humbling, amazing, and life-changing. Watching the interdependency of community and the way these people took care of their Elders, family, neighbors, friends, and us as their guests was truly awesome and inspiring.

Using the common denominator of food, we are learning from our past and focusing on the future, with the recognition that cultural evolution is imperative.

Barack Obama's place-card holder for his Anchorage dinner. ROB KINNEEN

MEAT AND GAME

COFFEE-AND-CREOLE-SPICED REINDEER LOIN WITH SPRUCE TIP SALT FINISH

MAKES 2 TO 4 SERVINGS

In 2013, at the request of Kawerak Reindeer Herders Association, I was selected to go to Washington, DC. Our goal was to raise awareness by Congress, the Bureau of Land Management, and other parties of interest about reindeer herding in Alaska.

I committed to cook USDA-approved reindeer from Alaska. Locating a kitchen proved challenging. Exhausting what seemed to be all avenues, I was figuring out how to cook on a hibachi on Pennsylvania Avenue. DC Central Kitchen came to my rescue, and I was able to use one of their facilities to prepare the reindeer. I also hired them to embellish the other aspects of the catering that were needed.

Reindeer is closely related to caribou, and yields rich, lean meat. Reindeer are herbivores and roam for food in northern climates. The meat is very nutritionally beneficial, as reindeers eat hearty grass, roots, and lichen.

During a preparatory visit to Anchorage, I met Bruce and Ann Davis of Midnite Sun Reindeer Ranch in Nome. Bruce is a third-generation reindeer rancher, and Ann has been perfecting her skills in tanning and tufting hides for purses, bags, and other items adorned with bone and horn. Their goal is to harvest the whole reindeer, making use of the meat, bones, and skin in traditional ways. They offer local meat in a hard-to-reach area of the state, where most items are shipped in.

The rich mix of Creole spice and coffee hold up well to the minerally, iron-y meat. I finished with Alaska Pure Spruce Tip Sea Salt. The spruce tip salt has hints of mint and rosemary. While geographically the reindeer and the spruce tree might not cross paths, this whole dish is completely Alaskan!

INGREDIENTS

- 1 pound reindeer loin, free of connective tissues (or lamb rack)
- 3 tablespoons Creole spice
- 2 teaspoons espresso grind of Alaska coffee (Steam Dot, Caldera Blend is good)
- ½ teaspoon kosher salt
- 3 tablespoons canola oil

PROCEDURE

1. Remove reindeer loin from the refrigerator 10 minutes before cooking.
2. With a paper towel, gently dab the excess moisture from the loin.
3. In a bowl, mix together Creole spice, salt, and coffee.
4. Coat the loin with the mixture on all sides.
5. In a pan over medium-high heat, heat the oil and add the reindeer loin. To avoid being splashed with the oil, be sure to set the meat down in the pan facing away from you.
6. Cook 1 minute per side.
7. Once cooked on all sides, pull from pan and check the temperature. It should read 115–120°F on a meat thermometer.
8. Let the meat rest for 5 minutes. During that time, the meat should carry over to 125–130°F. The idea is to serve medium rare but not raw. Slice very thin with a sharp knife and enjoy.
9. Serve with crackers as an appetizer or over olive oil mashed potatoes and roasted vegetables as an entrée.

CREOLE SPICE (BAMNATION!)

MAKES 10 TABLESPOONS

My first job out of culinary school was in New Orleans, Louisiana. I worked at NOLA, Emeril Lagasse's second restaurant. We used to make a huge batch of this monthly (about 40 pounds).

There are a lot of variations for Creole spice, and different varieties for seafood, game, poultry, and everything else. I have always quite liked this version—it is not too hot or sweet, and rounds out dishes with a nice pep.

It's affectionately referred to as Bamnation, yet I can't quite recall where that name came from. You get the idea.

INGREDIENTS

2½ tablespoons paprika

2 tablespoons kosher salt

2 tablespoons garlic powder

1 tablespoon black pepper

1 tablespoon onion powder

1 tablespoon dried oregano

1 teaspoon dried thyme

1 teaspoon cayenne

PROCEDURE

1. Measure and mix together.
2. Keep in glass jar for storage.

ELK ROLLED MEATLOAF

MAKES 8 TO 10 SERVINGS

This was inspired directly out of the foam-green recipe card file box at my house growing up! The canned asparagus was replaced with fresh veggies, the American cheese with grated cheddar. Over the years, it's been on menus and had a starring role on *Traditional Foods, Contemporary Chef*, a webisode series highlighting traditional foods in contemporary recipes.

This is a recipe best made for a gathering. It can be made ahead of time and heated up, and the presentation is pretty commanding. So just sit back and let it shine! Serve with Dandelion Pesto Potatoes (see page 49).

INGREDIENTS

5 pounds Alaska ground elk meat (or lean beef)

2 cups breadcrumbs (can use gluten-free panko)

2½ cups milk

⅓ cup tomato paste

1 bunch fresh parsley, minced

1 teaspoon ground black pepper

1 tablespoon chopped garlic

⅓ cup olive oil

2 yellow onions, quartered (2 cups)

3 carrots, cut into 2-inch-long segments (2 cups)

1 parsnip, cut into 2-inch-long segments (1 cup)

2 cups broccoli crowns, blanched and chopped

4 cups shredded cheddar

1 cup ketchup

⅓ cup Sriracha

PROCEDURE

1. Preheat oven to 350°F.
2. Mix the breadcrumbs, milk, tomato paste, herbs, black pepper, and garlic in a small bowl and set aside.
3. Toss the onions, carrots, and parsnip in olive oil, then roast in the oven until soft, about 15 to 20 minutes.
4. Blanch broccoli in boiling water for 45 seconds.
5. When the vegetables are cool, roughly chop them either by hand or in a food processor.
6. In a bowl, mix breadcrumb mixture into the meat by hand.
7. Line a sheet pan with plastic wrap.
8. Spread the meat mixture on the lined pan, leaving about 3 inches at one end of the pan uncovered.
9. Spread the chopped vegetables over the meat, leaving a 1-inch border on all four sides. Sprinkle cheese all over, lightly pressing it into the meat.
10. Pull the plastic from the edges, and use it to help roll the meat over the vegetables and cheese, with the long part of the pan facing you, creating a roulade. Don't roll the plastic into the meatloaf!
11. Transfer the roll to another sheet pan, this time lined with parchment paper. Place the rolled edge down at an angle, and secure the paper with a fork. Be sure to remove all plastic from the meatloaf before baking.
12. In a small bowl, mix the Sriracha and ketchup. Pour this over the top of the meatloaf.
13. Bake in the oven 25 minutes, or until 160°F internal temperature is achieved.
14. Cut into 1-inch-thick portions and serve each person two slices.
15. Serve with Dandelion Pesto Potatoes (see page 49).

ASH ADAMS

ALASKA GAME SKEWERS WITH ALASKA BERRY-BIRCH SYRUP VINAIGRETTE OVER FIDDLEHEADS AND BROWN RICE

MAKES 4 SERVINGS

I prepared this recipe for Al Roker when he visited Alaska for *The Today Show*. He seemed to genuinely enjoy these fresh takes on regional Alaska fare, and it was really exciting to talk about beach asparagus, fiddleheads, spruce tips, and Alaska birch syrup with a national audience.

This recipe is region-specific. In the event you cannot find spruce tips, substitute rosemary. For beach asparagus and fiddleheads, I recommend regular asparagus or something that celebrates summer where you are. For birch syrup, try using maple or sorghum.

INGREDIENTS FOR SKEWERS

1 pound elk or bison loin. For each skewer, cut into ¾-inch cubes (need 4 pieces per skewer).

1 red pepper, cut into ½-inch cubes, need 16 pieces

1 onion, cut into ½-inch wedges, need 16 pieces

1 zucchini, cut into ½-inch rings, need 16 pieces

4 12-inch skewer sticks, soaked in water

INGREDIENTS FOR MEAT MARINADE

¼ teaspoon shredded spruce tips (similar to rosemary)

Pinch red pepper flakes

¼ teaspoon olive oil

¼ teaspoon minced garlic

½ lemon, zested then juiced

PROCEDURE FOR SKEWERS

1. Mix marinade ingredients together.
2. Add meat, then marinate for 1 hour.
3. Skewer meat, onion, pepper, meat, then zucchini. Repeat with 4 pieces of meat.
4. Place meat on medium high grill for 1 minute on each side.
5. Let rest for 3 minutes after removing from the grill.

INGREDIENTS FOR BROWN RICE

1 cup water

½ cup brown rice

PROCEDURE FOR BROWN RICE

1. Bring water to a boil, add rice, and stir.
2. Drop to a simmer and cover.
3. Let cook for 25 minutes, or until most of the water has been absorbed and the rice is tender to the bite.
4. Remove from heat and keep covered for 10 minutes.

INGREDIENTS FOR VEGETABLES

¼ cup vegetable oil

1 cup fiddleheads, foraged

1 cup beach asparagus

Kosher salt

PROCEDURE FOR VEGETABLES

1. Heat a sauté pan to medium heat, then add oil and vegetables.
2. Sauté for 1 minute.
3. Season with salt and set aside.

INGREDIENTS FOR VINAIGRETTE

¼ cup water

1 cup Alaska cranberries

1 tablespoon birch syrup

2 tablespoons balsamic vinegar

1 teaspoon Dijon mustard

6 tablespoons vegetable oil

PROCEDURE FOR VINAIGRETTE

1. Bring water to boil, then add birch syrup, cranberries, cook for 3 minutes, turn off
2. Let it cool.
3. Add in the vinegar and mustard, puree for 30 seconds. Slowly drizzle oil into the mix with an immersion blender.
4. Will keep for a week in the refrigerator.

PROCEDURE FOR PLATING

1. Place mound of brown rice in the center of a platter.
2. Arrange vegetables on top.
3. Drip the berry vinaigrette around the well of the platter.
4. Place the skewers on the mound of rice.

MOROCCAN-SPICED UMPQUA VALLEY LAMB CHOPS OVER MATANUSKA VALLEY CARROT PUREE AND SPRUCE TIP SYRUP

MAKES 4 SERVINGS

I contributed this recipe to *Pacific Feast*, by Jennifer Hahn. At the time I was working as chef at a Mediterranean restaurant in Anchorage. The owner had a great connection with Umpqua lamb, which is sourced out of Oregon.

Alaska carrots are super sweet due to the long days and short nights in the summer, so adjust the carrots with a sweetener if needed.

INGREDIENTS FOR MOROCCAN SPICE

- 1½ teaspoons crushed red pepper
- 3 teaspoons whole caraway seed
- 2 teaspoons whole cumin seed
- 6 teaspoons whole coriander seed
- 3 teaspoons peppercorns
- 2 teaspoons dried mint
- 3 teaspoons kosher salt
- 3 teaspoons brown sugar

PROCEDURE FOR MOROCCAN SPICE

1. In a spice grinder, or with a mortar and pestle, grind the whole seeds and peppercorns.
2. Fold in crushed red pepper with the mint, salt, and brown sugar.

INGREDIENTS FOR MATANUSKA VALLEY CARROT PUREE

- 1 pound carrots, peeled and diced in ½-inch pieces, preferably from the Matanuska Valley or your local farmers market
- 2 tablespoons unsalted butter
- ½ cup water or apple juice
- Salt and pepper

PROCEDURE FOR MATANUSKA VALLEY CARROT PUREE

1. Preheat oven to 350°F.
2. Add all ingredients in an ovenproof pan and cover with foil. Bake for 30 minutes or until carrots are easily pierced with a fork.
3. Puree with an immersion blender.
4. Finish with salt and pepper.

INGREDIENTS FOR UMPQUA VALLEY LAMB

1½ pounds lamb chops, free of connective tissue, in 4-ounce portions

¼ cup Moroccan Spice Mix (see page 96)

2 tablespoons olive oil

PROCEDURE FOR UMPQUA VALLEY LAMB

1. Remove chops from the refrigerator 10 minutes before cooking.
2. Brush with olive oil, and coat with Moroccan Spice Mix.
3. On a preheated grill or in a pan over medium heat, sear each side for 4 to 6 minutes.
4. Let the lamb rest for 2 minutes to reach an internal temperature of 125°F.

INGREDIENTS FOR SPRUCE TIP SYRUP

Recipe created by Dave and JoAnn Lesh, Gustavus Inn, Gustavus, Alaska.

4 cups spruce tips

4 cups water

⅔ cup sugar

PROCEDURE FOR SPRUCE TIP SYRUP

1. In a medium saucepan, bring water and spruce tips to a boil, reduce heat, and simmer for 15 minutes.
2. Strain, put the spruce tips back in the pot, add sugar, and reduce to a syrup consistency.

TO PLATE

1. Place 2 ounces of puree in the center of a plate.
2. Place the lamb chop in the middle of the puree.
3. Drizzle with 2 tablespoons of spruce tip syrup.

ASH ADAMS

NOBLE'S DELIGHT, FEATURING ALASKA REINDEER

MAKES 2 ENTRÉES OR 4 APPETIZERS

I vividly remember going into my uncle's garage and seeing a few dozen deer aging after hunting season. They were his, my family's, and other hunting buddies'. We grew up not really realizing how expensive meat truly was.

When we moved to Anchorage, I remember a few failed family attempts at hunting. Eventually my interests were directed toward urban adventures, and I elected to stay home from the weekend hunting trips.

One memorable year, my family came back with two moose! But as the steaks and roasts disappeared, so did the excitement. To meet the challenge, we concocted a dutiful dinner of deluxe macaroni and cheese, and ground moose meat, for the long winter.

Years later, when I was making family meals in restaurants, I started making a mac and cheese dish with caramelized onions and ground leftover meat. It took me a little while to remember where the inspiration came from!

When my diner came to fruition, I knew I would name the dish after my grandpa, Noble. I do not believe he ever experienced our dinner devoted to ground moose with mac and cheese, but it just seemed right.

If you hunt or practice whole animal butchery, you know the massive grind that comes from the animal. If you are selling this in a restaurant, you will have to purchase the meat. Reindeer, elk, bison, or beef will work as well. We chose to highlight reindeer for this reason.

Topping with a balsamic dressing is a great way to cut the richness of the sauce and the sweetness of the onions.

INGREDIENTS

- ¾ pound cooked penne pasta (6 ounces raw pasta), prepared per instructions
- 2 tablespoons vegetable oil
- ½ cup ground reindeer (or other lean meat)
- ½ cup caramelized onions
- 1 cup béchamel sauce (see page 100)
- 1 cup vegetable stock or milk, (2 oz for deglazing; reserve the rest to adjust the sauce if needed)
- ½ cup cheddar cheese
- 1 cup raw spinach
- ¼ cup balsamic vinaigrette

PROCEDURE

1. In a pan over medium-high heat, add oil and ground meat. Brown and cook halfway.
2. Add the caramelized onions and stir in.
3. Warm through, and deglaze with 2 ounces stock or milk. When it comes to a bubble, add the béchamel and cheddar. Stir.
4. As everything is warming through, add the cooked pasta, and season with salt. Mix gently. If the sauce is getting too thick, use the reserved milk to thin it out a touch.
5. Plate the pasta.

BÉCHAMEL SAUCE

MAKES 1 PINT

The roux-to-milk ratio is pretty low; I used to make it very thick, but over time found the dish too heavy and wanted to thin it out a bit.

As this sauce will be reheated and have cheese added to it, it is good to start with the béchamel a little lighter.

INGREDIENTS

2 tablespoons flour

2 tablespoons unsalted butter

2 cups milk

1 bay leaf

PROCEDURE

1. In a medium-size nonreactive pan, melt butter and add flour.
2. Cook over medium-low heat until the butter and flour are combined and look like wet sand. Cook to a blond state (it will offer viscosity to the milk and subtle flavor).
3. Add the milk in slowly, in thirds. Throw the bay leaf in as well.
4. Stir continuously and make sure the heat is medium low.
5. Cook until the milk thickens up and coats the back of a spoon.

CARAMELIZED ONIONS

MAKES 1 CUP

My first job out of culinary school was in New Orleans at NOLA restaurant. I learned about myself as a young man down there, and a thing or two about cooking as well.

We would have to cut three five-gallon buckets of onions three times a week to make caramelized onions. There are shortcuts like balsamic vinegar and sugar, but none of them hold a candle to coaxing the sweet, subtle, sugary love from these pungent devils.

INGREDIENTS

¼ cup vegetable oil

2 pounds yellow onions, julienne

¾ teaspoon salt

1 cup water (as needed)

PROCEDURE

1. In a medium-size saucepan, add oil, a third of the onions, and ¼ teaspoon salt.
2. Stir constantly. When you start to notice that the onions are looking glassy or translucent, turn the heat down a touch and continue to stir.
3. If you notice any sticking, add a tablespoon of water to deglaze the pot. This should take about 15 minutes for the first third. If at any time there is a fond building on the bottom of the pan, turn off the heat and cover fond with the onions. Let the onions sit for about 5 to 10 minutes. The fond will lift and not scorch, and the flavor will be amazing.
4. Add the next third of the onions and ¼ teaspoon salt to the pot. Stir and add the residual liquid to deglaze.
5. Add the final third amount of onions with the last ¼ teaspoon of salt.
6. When the onions are a deep brown color and all the residual liquid has been evaporated, they should be done.
7. The volume of the onions should decrease by half.
8. Take off heat and let cool.
9. Store in covered container for up to one week.

RED BEANS AND RICE WITH REINDEER SAUSAGE

MAKES 8 TO 12 SERVINGS

I opened Noble's Diner in Anchorage in 2004. Up to this point, my experience had been in upscale restaurants. Noble's focused on serving local fare in an accessible and casual way.

By this time, I had New Orleans and North Carolina under my belt, so I leaned on traditional Southern dishes made with local Alaska ingredients.

We limped along for three years and finally put a fork in it. While we were not successful financially, it was a humbling and beautiful experience. This dish was on the menu, and it seems elementary now, but I really like the flavors and message it conveyed for merging local food with traditional fare—even if you have to borrow the recipe! Indian Valley Meats makes the best reindeer sausage around. If you cannot find that, please substitute a rich game sausage or chorizo.

INGREDIENTS

- 2½ pounds small red beans
- 1 gallon water
- ¼ cup vegetable oil
- 3 pounds of reindeer sausage,* cut into ½-inch pieces (recommended: Indian Valley Meats mild Polish reindeer sausage)
- 1 yellow onion, medium dice
- ½ bunch celery, medium dice
- 2 red peppers, medium dice
- ¼ cup minced garlic
- ½ cup Creole Spice Mix (see page 91)
- 2 12-ounce cans Alaska-brewed pale ale
- 1½ cups tomato puree
- ⅓ cup Worcestershire sauce
- ¼ cup Tabasco
- 12 cups water
- 2 cups brown rice

**You can substitute chorizo for reindeer sausage*

PROCEDURE FOR RED BEANS

1. In a large pot, add the beans and cover with a gallon of water.
2. Bring to a boil, turn off heat, and cover for 1 hour. This is a hot soak. It will evenly and quickly bloom a bean for a more uniform cooking time.
3. In a thick-gauged, medium-size pot over medium heat, render the reindeer sausage with oil.
4. When browned, add onion, celery, and peppers. Cook until translucent.
5. Finish with garlic and Creole Spice Mix. Stir for 45 seconds.
6. Deglaze with the Alaska beer, then add remaining ingredients.
7. Bring to a boil, drop to a simmer, and cook until beans are tender.

PROCEDURE FOR RICE

1. Rinse brown rice, and set aside.
2. Bring 4 cups of water to a boil in a thick-bottomed pot with a tight-fitting lid.
3. Add rice, stir, bring back to a boil, then drop to a simmer.
4. Cook on low heat for 35 minutes.
5. Turn off heat and let steam for 10 to 15 more minutes.
6. When finished, fluff with a fork.

WILD DUCK RISOTTO

MAKES 2 ENTRÉES OR 4 APPETIZERS

This recipe was written at an Athabascan Elder's homestead on the Tanana River. It was prepped in a chow hall and cooked over propane on cast iron. While I was collaborating with the webisode series *Traditional Foods, Contemporary Chef*, we would seldom have a concrete plan for what to prepare. We wanted food from the region, which depended on seasonality and the kindness of people we were visiting.

Troth, or Indian potato, is a root that is usually saved for dessert. I knew the sweetness would hold up to the wild duck. Wild duck is far more minerally, or iron-tasting, than domestic duck. The muscles tend to be smaller and more compact as well.

The duck broth was literally all the veggie scraps and the carcass simmering over the fire for two hours. After that, I seared the duck meat and deglazed with the broth. Apple juice or low-sodium chicken stock can be used as a substitute.

INGREDIENTS

¼ cup vegetable oil
½ cup small-diced onion
½ cup small-diced carrot
1 cup Alaska Flour Company whole barley
3 cups duck broth
1 cup duck meat, cooked and chopped into pieces
1 cup medium-diced winter squash
¼ cup Indian potato (troth), skinned and sliced into small pieces (omit if not able to source)
½ cup kale, cut into ribbons
2 tablespoons butter

PROCEDURE

1. In a 3-quart pot over medium-high heat, add vegetable oil followed by the onion and carrots, and stir. After 1 minute, add the barley.
2. When vegetables are translucent, add the squash and troth.
3. Deglaze with one cup of the broth and stir.
4. Stir frequently and add a cup of broth at a time. When there is about a third of the broth left, add the cooked duck meat and ribbons of greens.
5. When everything is incorporated, remove from heat and add butter. This will cause it to incorporate, rather than ooze out as an oily mess.

BRIAN ADAMS

DESSERTS AND BEVERAGES

ASH ADAMS

The diversity of Alaska brings us different items for dessert from all across the state. Some are classic ingredients, such as berries and rhubarb. From an indigenous point of view, troth—a sweet root found in the interior and northern areas—is also popular. Berries translate well here, as do Labrador tea, spruce tips, birch syrup, and coffee.

Some of my favorite flavors are made at Kahiltna Birchworks in Talkeetna, Alaska. Dulce and Michael East have been producing syrups and natural botanical preserves for upwards of twenty years. They are resourceful folks who use the natural bounty of Alaska—birch sap for syrup, berries for jams, jellies, and sauces. Most recently they have started processing chaga, a fungus that grows on birch trees and has been used by the Athabascan people for thousands of years as an anti-inflammatory believed to aid in fighting cancer.

For the last two decades, between late April and May when the birch sap runs, Dulce and Michael have collected and reduced it. One hundred gallons of sap makes a single gallon of syrup, one of the rarer products in the world. If you get your hands on some, savor it and enjoy!

Michael and Dulce East harvesting birch sap. PHOTO COURTESY MICHAEL AND DULCE EAST.

PHOTO COURTESY MICHAEL AND DULCE EAST.

AGUDAK

MAKES 4 TO 6 SERVINGS

Depending on where in Alaska you are, there are many different variations on the recipe for agudak (pronounced *ah-goo-dak*; aqutaq in Yup'ik spelling), also known as Indian ice cream or Eskimo ice cream.

More northern and interior regions used caribou or moose tallow (fat). Areas next to the sea would use whale or seal fat. Over time, Crisco has taken on a commanding role in this recipe. I like this version, as it has lots of fish and berries, and Crisco is more of a binder than a main ingredient.

Evelyn Elliott showed me this version, which includes using whitefish. Evelyn is from Bethel, a town in the Yukon-Kuskokwim region of Southwest Alaska. Whitefish is a subsistence river fish that has a flaky, neutral texture. I would recommend using cod for a similar result, as it has flaky flesh and a more neutral flavor than other Alaska white fish.

While fish, berries, sugar, and fat for dessert may not be in culinary vogue at the moment, this dish is very much alive in Alaska. You will more than likely see agudak on the table at weddings, birthdays, potlucks, funerals, and other celebrations. I have used this recipe myself at Alaska-centric events.

Evelyn showed me this recipe when I catered the National Indian Health Board Culture Night in 2011. There were five hundred attendees from the circumpolar region and the United States, and I was honored to prepare food from around the state to highlight the many regions of Alaska. For me, this represents the resourcefulness and resilience of Alaska's people. More than likely, agudak began as a way to preserve berries beyond the summer.

INGREDIENTS

- 8 ounces white-fleshed fish (preferably Alaska cod)
- 2 cups water
- ½ cup Crisco
- ½ cup sugar
- 1 cup (5 ounces) frozen raspberries
- 1 cup (6 ounces) frozen blueberries

PROCEDURE

1. Bring the water and fish to a boil, drop to a simmer, and cook until the fish is poached. Cook through until it flakes apart, about 7 to 10 minutes.
2. Strain the water and reserve. Let the fish cool for about 5 minutes.
3. In a tabletop mixer using the whisk attachment, add fish, Crisco, and sugar, and whip until it all incorporates and aerates, about 2 to 3 minutes.
4. Add the reserved liquid sparingly to assist with aeration, about 2 to 4 ounces on average.
5. Add the berries last, and pulse.
6. My personal preference is to have the berries bleed into the agudak, leaving some whole berries for texture.

Helpful Hint: There are many different variables to this recipe, including the type of fish used, the sweetness of the berries, and how much vegetable shortening you want to use. So please taste, feel, and look to make sure you get the result you want.

ASH ADAMS

FRY BREAD WITH LABRADOR TEA AND CRANBERRIES

MAKES 8 SERVINGS

I developed this recipe for the Alaska Native Health Consortium *Traditional Foods, Contemporary Chef* webisode series. Fry bread has a pretty negative connotation in contemporary contexts. Dietitians tend to really dislike the nutritional components (since it, um, doesn't have any). The fact that it's really a food that grew from government commodities offered in oppressive environments doesn't help. But by adding a few redeeming ingredients and keeping it for a snack or treat does tend to make this a little more center of the road.

This webisode was shot at an Athabascan Elder's homestead on the Tanana River right outside of Fairbanks. The whole weekend we were cooking with propane and fire outdoors with the beautiful Tanana River as a backdrop. I first attempted to make this on the grill, but the alternative flours did not want to agree with me! I am proud of this recipe and the dialogue it now spurs—reminding us of history, but also that we can add ingredients to make some of our foods better.

INGREDIENTS

1 cup chickpea flour

1 cup brown rice flour

2 cups all-purpose flour

2 teaspoons baking powder

½ teaspoon kosher salt

2 tablespoons Labrador tea*

½ cup Alaska cranberries

1½ cups warm water

2 cups vegetable oil

**Please recognize that Labrador tea is used as both food and medicine historically. Please practice moderation when consuming.*

PROCEDURE

1. Mix the flours, salt, and baking powder.
2. Add the wet ingredients.
3. Fold in the berries and tea.
4. Cook over medium heat, pan-frying in a ½-inch of vegetable oil until golden brown, and flip.
5. Drain on paper towel. Enjoy!

BRIAN ADAMS

ASH ADAMS

BIRCH SYRUP CRÈME BRÛLÉE

MAKES 6 SERVINGS

I'd like you all to meet Charles Baki. Chas Baki, Chaswick the Entertainer, Chasinart, Chasimoto . . . Chas.

A good-time guy with Sideshow Bob hair, perma-smile, and easy demeanor, Chas came into my life when I had my diner. He was one of the essential people who helped us limp along for a few years, and his dedication to the place was second to none. Though he filled many roles, he started as a baker. I wasn't interested in creating desserts that you could find all over town, so I had a real issue when he showed me a crème brûlée. Until I tasted it, that is! The unique flavor of the birch syrup was really addictive and popular through the life of Noble's Diner—so thanks, Chas!

I use Kahiltna Birch Syrup. Be sure to use medium-grade, as the lighter grades are for pancakes and such, and the darker grade can be too overpowering.

And Chas? He is now an upstanding citizen in the Midwest with a beautiful family.

INGREDIENTS

3 cups heavy cream
1½ cup half-and-half
9 egg yolks
1 cup sugar
1 cup birch syrup
1 teaspoon vanilla
Natural brown sugar (turbinado or Sugar in the Raw) for brûlée

PROCEDURE

1. Combine cream with half-and-half in saucepan, and bring to a boil.
2. While the mix is coming to a boil, in a large bowl whip up yolks and sugar until combined.
3. Temper the egg-sugar mix by slowly adding 6 ounces of cream at a time.
4. Once all combined, pour into 6 8-ounce ramekins. Place the ramekins into a pan with edges that can hold water up to halfway on the ramekins.
5. Bake at 325°F (no fan) for 40 minutes, or until the middle is set but still jiggles. After 40 minutes, if extra time is needed, check every 8 to 10 minutes.
6. When the brûlée is set, remove from oven and pan, and set out for 15 minutes. When cool enough to handle, set in the refrigerator for at least four hours.
7. When serving, top with raw sugar, coating evenly but not too liberally. Cook with a torch, melting the sugar to leave a crispy top. Serve immediately.
8. If you do not have a torch or don't know how to use one, please serve with berries on top as pots de crème.

ICED CHAGA WITH BIRCH SYRUP

MAKES 4 SERVINGS

Chaga is a protective fungus that forms on birch trees after a branch breaks. Used by Athabascan people for thousands of years as a cure-all, its beneficial properties have been known to aid inflammation, boost the immune system, regulate the digestive track, and provide nutritional support in fighting cancer. While technically a fungus, it has a flavor that is earthier with slight hints of vanilla.

To prepare the chaga, it is harvested from living trees and ground into a powder to steep in boiling water.

Birch syrup is the product of birch sap returning in the spring to replenish the birch trees. Harvested much like maple, it is then concentrated in a sugar shack. While it takes forty gallons of sap to make one gallon of maple syrup, a single gallon of birch sap requires 100 gallons of sap!

I like to brew this up to create a uniquely Alaska beverage at caterings.

I have also used this to deglaze pork chops and finish with butter . . . but that might be for another time.

Please enjoy this recipe knowing you are drinking a tasty beverage that is actually good for you on many levels.

INGREDIENTS

4 cups water

5 tablespoons chaga*

¼ cup birch syrup or to taste

**Chaga is a living fungus that is meant to protect a damaged tree. If harvesting, please only remove ¼ of the fungus so the tree will be able to regenerate and there is more for others to harvest.*

PROCEDURE

1. Add the chaga to the water, bring it to a boil, and reduce to simmer.
2. Cook for 2 hours, and add water as needed to refill.
3. After 2 hours, add birch syrup and stir.
4. When cool enough to handle, strain and cool.
5. Serve over ice.

PARSNIP CAKE WITH SPRUCE TIP CREMA

MAKES 4 TO 6 SERVINGS

In the Land of the Midnight Sun, there is no shortage of roots or tubers. Parsnips are a bit more fickle than carrots; they don't last as long in root storage, so there are only select farmers who make the effort. Parsnips are spicy and sweet, and their flavor compounds after baking. It might seem like there is allspice, nutmeg, and more in there, but nope—just a sassy parsnip!

I first created this dessert for a visiting New Orleans chef. He was enamored with the spruce tip flavor, which is not too common in the bayou. Spruce tips have a rosemary-mint taste on the finish. Delicious!

INGREDIENTS FOR PARSNIP CAKE

2 cups all-purpose flour
2 teaspoons baking soda
2 teaspoons baking powder
½ teaspoon iodized salt
3 teaspoons cinnamon
2 teaspoons vanilla
1 cup granulated sugar
1 cup brown sugar
4 eggs
1¼ cup vegetable oil
3 cups grated parsnip

PROCEDURE FOR PARSNIP CAKE

1. Turn low-fan convection oven to 350°F, or preheat a regular oven with no fan to 375°F.
2. In a bowl add flour, baking soda, baking powder, iodized salt, and cinnamon. Mix and sift.
3. With a tabletop mixer, combine sugar and vanilla together then turn mixer to low. Add one egg at a time to incorporate slowly, then add the oil.
4. Once all wet ingredients are incorporated, fold in the flour one-third at a time. Last, add in the grated parsnip, making sure not to overmix.
5. I use two terrine molds. Butter and flour the pans before adding the mix. You can also use a 9-by-13 sheet pan.
6. Cook for 30 minutes, and check every 5 minutes until done. It can take up to 40 minutes total. Poke a toothpick in the center of the pan; it will come out clean when the cake is done.
7. Set on a cooling rack.
8. Once cool, top with spruce tip crema and berries.

INGREDIENTS FOR SPRUCE TIP CREMA

½ cup water
¼ cup sugar
¼ cup chopped spruce tips
1 cup heavy whipping cream

PROCEDURE FOR SPRUCE TIP CREMA

1. Boil water with sugar to dissolve.
2. Add spruce tips, and remove from heat to cool.
3. In a separate bowl, whip cream into soft peaks.
4. Fold in one tablespoon of spruce tip syrup.

RHUBARB-BERRY AGUA FRESCA

MAKES 12 8-OUNCE PORTIONS

This drink recipe was originally written for Barrow, Alaska, a wonderful town on the edge of the Arctic Ocean, now officially known by its Iñupiaq name of Utqiaġvik. There are community-minded messages on dumpsters around town. One message screams "Stop the Pop."

Barrow is a town of 4,500 today, but it has been an Iñupiat community for thousands of years. While there is a harsh winter climate, they do have seasons rich with berries and other flora. There is an effort to modify diets away from commodity and convenience foods and back to what nature intended.

I can get behind that, but I also have never been happy with being told "No" or "Don't." This recipe was written to offer an alternative to soda. Parents can control the sugar content of this beverage.

INGREDIENTS

3 cups water

1 cup sugar

1 pound rhubarb, cut into 3-inch sticks

½ pound Alaska berries, your choice

6 cups sparkling water, recommend soda water

PROCEDURE

1. Combine sugar and water in a small saucepan and bring to a boil.
2. Add the rhubarb sticks to the water and sugar mixture, then remove from heat to steep.
3. When the rhubarb mixture is cool, pour off the rhubarb-infused liquid. Reserve the remaining candied rhubarb and enough liquid to keep the pieces covered to use as a garnish later.
4. Mix the rhubarb infusion with berries in a stainless steel pot.
5. Bring to a boil, and then remove from heat.
6. Puree, either with an immersion blender or by transferring the liquid to a standard blender or food processor.
7. Strain through a fine sieve or cheesecloth to remove seeds.
8. Adjust sweetness to taste with maple syrup or sugar.

TO SERVE

1. To make 2 servings, combine 1 cup rhubarb-berry mixture with 2 cups sparkling water.
2. Garnish with several pieces of the reserved rhubarb.

Note: To store candied rhubarb, refrigerate submerged in cooking liquid in an airtight container for up to 7 days.

ASH ADAMS

RHUBARB CLAFOUTIS WITH WHIPPED SPRUCE TIP CREMA

MAKES 4 SERVINGS

I had the opportunity to cook a multicourse dinner for the executive chef of the Food Network while he was visiting Anchorage. A pretty good menu was composed, I must say, but I was hung up on the dessert, as it is not my forte. On my way to work, I grabbed a few stalks of rhubarb out of my garden, on the fly. Clafoutis is a traditional dessert highlighting the tart cherries from the south of France. I took some liberties to make an Alaskafied version with rhubarb and spruce tip crema, which I think is pretty much perfect!

INGREDIENTS FOR BATTER

½ cup all-purpose flour
¼ teaspoon kosher salt
2 eggs
2 tablespoons brown sugar
¾ cup milk
1 tablespoon melted butter

INGREDIENTS FOR FRUIT BASE

1 cup rhubarb, cut into ½-inch pieces
2 tablespoons butter
2 tablespoons brown sugar

PROCEDURE FOR CLAFOUTIS

1. Preheat oven to 425°F.
2. Mix the batter ingredients together, and set aside.
3. Over medium heat in a non-aluminum pan, melt butter and brown sugar.
4. Add rhubarb and cook for 1 minute, achieving a glaze.
5. Top the pan with the batter and put it into the oven.
6. Cook 10 to 12 minutes.
7. Serve with Spruce Tip Crema.

INGREDIENTS FOR SPRUCE TIP CREMA

½ cup water
¼ cup sugar
¼ cup chopped spruce tips
1 cup heavy whipping cream

PROCEDURE FOR SPRUCE TIP CREMA

1. Boil water with sugar to dissolve.
2. Add spruce tips and remove from heat to cool.
3. In a separate bowl whip cream into soft peaks.
4. Fold in one tablespoon of syrup.

BRIAN ADAMS

Agudak, 108
agudak (Eskimo ice cream), 2
Alaska
  Baranof Island Brewing Company, 46
  Barrow (Utqiaġvik), 27, 116
  Bristol Bay, 12, 55–57
  Center Market, Matanuska Valley, 78
  distilleries in, 19
  diversity of, 3–4, 107
  farmers markets, 8–9
  Favco (fishmonger), Anchorage, 12
  Flat Island community, 84
  growing season and produce of, 8–9
  Matanuska Valley, 8, 78
  Meyer Farms, 9
  miles of coastline, 60
  Mitkof Island, 2
  Nome, 2, 90
  seafood in, 60–61
  Sitka, 8, 46–47
  Tyonek, 8–9, 60
Alaska Berry-Birch Syrup Vinaigrette, 95
Alaska cod, in Agudak, 108
Alaska Escabeche with Tzatziki, 11
Alaska Flour Company, 36
Alaska Game Skewers with Alaska Berry-Birch Syrup Vinaigrette, 94–95
Alaska King Crab Oscar Bites with Béarnaise Aioli, 15–16
Alaska Oyster Shooter or Granita, 22
Alaska Oyster Shooter with Alder-Smoked Salt Rim and Alaskan Summer Ale, 23
Alaska Oysters Roasted with Reindeer Sausage and Spinach, 25
Alaska Pure Fireweed Honey, 76
Alaska Pure Spruce Tip Sea Salt, 90
Alaska Rose Hip Vinaigrette, 76
Alaska Salmon Head Pho, 44–45
Alaska Seafood Cakes with Apple Slaw, 12–13
Alaska Seafood Marketing Institute, 19
Alaska whitefish, 12
appetizers and snacks
  Alaska Escabeche with Tzatziki, 11
  Alaska King Crab Oscar Bites with Béarnaise Aioli, 15–16
  Alaska Oyster Shooter or Granita, 22
  Alaska Oyster Shooter with Alder-Smoked Salt Rim and Alaskan Summer Ale, 23
  Alaska Oysters Roasted with Reindeer Sausage and Spinach, 25
  Alaska Seafood Cakes with Apple Slaw, 12
  Apple Slaw, 13
  Beet and Vodka-Cured Alaska Salmon Gravlax, 19
  Fresh Rolls with Herring Eggs, Sea Asparagus and Lovage, 20
  Muktuk Sushi Roll with Local Bean Sprouts, 27
  Pan-Seared Alaska Snow Crab–Stuffed Risotto Cakes with Winter Salad, 28–29
  Razor Clam Fritters, 31
  Roasted Alaska Oysters, 23
  Smoked Salmon White Bean Crostini, 32
apples
  Apple Slaw, 13
  in winter salad, 29
aqua fresca, rhubarb-berry, 116
Arctic Shrimp and Grits with Bacon and Red-Eye Gravy, 62
asparagus, in Alaska Crab Oscar Bites, 15
author
  childhood on Mitkof Island, 2
  in "Tlingit bling" chef's jacket, 86

Bagna Cauda Vinaigrette, 51
Baki, Charles, 113
Baranof Island Brewing Company, 46
Barker, Ben and Karen, 50
barley, 36, 42
Barrow, Alaska (Utqiaġvik), 27, 116
beach asparagus, 20, 27, 69–70, 81, 94, 95
beach greens, 44, 70, 81
beach peas, 70
bean sprouts, 27, 45
Béarnaise Aioli, 16
Bear Trail Lodge, Bristol Bay, 57
Béchamel Sauce, 100
Beet and Vodka-Cured Alaska Salmon Gravlax, 19
beets
  pickled, 79
  in Roasted Root Veggies, 43
  in Toasted Quinoa-Root Vegetable Hash, 80
Bering Sea, 84, 86
berries
  in Alaska, 8–9, 107
  blueberries, 86, 108
  cranberries, 95, 110
  on Parsnip Cake with Spruce Tip Crema, 113
  on pots de crème, 113
  in Rhubarb-Berry Aqua Fresca, 116
  wild blueberries, 2
beverages
  Iced Chaga with Birch Syrup, 114
  Rhubarb-Berry Aqua Fresca, 116
birch syrup
  in Alaska Berry-Birch Syrup Vinaigrette, 95
  iced chaga with, 114
  Kahiltna Birchworks and, 107
  in Pan-Seared Alaska Halibut Cheeks in a Birch–Brown Butter Sauce, 75
Birch Syrup Crème Brûlée, 113
bison, 94
bladderwrack seaweed, in Foraged Fried Rice, 81
blanket toss, 2
blueberries
  in Agudak, 108
  in indigenized cuisine, 86
  wild, picking, 2
Boekmann, Adem, 61
Braised Rockfish with Fumet, Vegetables, Seaweed, and Seal Oil, 65–66

Bristol Bay Salmon over Foraged Rice Pasta and Tundra Vinaigrette, 69–70
brown rice
 with Alaska Game Skewers, 94–95
 in Red Beans and Rice with Reindeer Sausage, 102
 in Seared Rockfish over Shrimp and Foraged Fried Rice, 81
brown rice flour, in Fry Bread with Labrador Tea and Cranberries, 110

cabbage, 13
Caramelized Onions, 101
carrots
 in Alaska Salmon Head Pho, 45
 in Elk Rolled Meatloaf, 92
 in foraged fried rice, 81
 in Fresh Rolls, 20
 growing conditions in Matanuska Valley, 78
 Matanuska Valley Carrot Puree, 96
 in Muktuk Sushi Roll, 27
 in Roasted Root Veggies, 43
 in Toasted Quinoa-Root Vegetable Hash, 80
 in Wild Duck Risotto, 103
Caswell, Seth, 47
Center Market, Matanuska Valley, 78
ceviche, 11
chaga, 107, 114
chard, 45
Chicken Stock, 53
chickpea flour, in Fry Bread, 110
clafoutis, 119
Clams and Sausage in a White Wine Broth, 72
climate change, 87
cod
 in Agudak, 108
 House-Made Salt Cod, 74
Coffee-and-Creole-Spiced Reindeer Loin with Spruce-Tip Salt Finish, 90–91
cold-weather farming techniques, 9
Community Development Quota Program, 61
community farm, Tyonek, 8–9
Corn Soup with Three Sisters Salsa, 38
crab
 Alaska King Crab Oscar Bites with Béarnaise Aioli, 15–16
 Pan-Seared Alaska Snow Crab–Stuffed Risotto Cakes, 28–29
Crab and Shrimp Stock, 52
 in crab-stuffed risotto cakes, 28–29
crackers, 32, 86
cranberries, 95, 110
Cream of Barley Breakfast Cereal, in Arctic Grits or Northern Polenta, 36
Creole Spice (Bamnation!), 91
 in Arctic Shrimp and Grits, 62
 in Red Beans and Rice with Reindeer Sausage, 102
Crisco, in Agudak, 108
crostini
 Smoked Salmon White Bean Crostini, 32
cucumbers
 in Alaska Oyster Shooter, 23
 in Muktuk Sushi Roll, 27
 in Tzatziki, 51

daikon radish
 in Alaska Salmon Head Pho, 45
 in Foraged Fried Rice, 81
 in Roasted Root Veggies, 43
Dandelion Pesto Potatoes, 49
Davis, Alex, 78
Davis, Ann and Bruce, 90
Davis, Clarence, 2
DC Central Kitchen, Washington, D.C., 90
Denkler, Glenn, 2
desserts
 Agudak, 108
 Birch Syrup Crème Brûlée, 113
 Fry Bread with Labrador Tea and Cranberries, 110
 Parsnip Cake with Spruce Tip Crema, 115
 pots de crème, 113
 Rhubarb Clafoutis with Whipped Spruce Tip Crema, 119
distilleries in Alaska, 19
duck, wild, 103
duck broth, 103

East, Dulce and Michael, 107
elk, in Alaska Game Skewers, 94
Elk Rolled Meatloaf, 92
Elliott, Evelyn, 108
escabeche with tzatziki, 11

farmers markets, 8–9
Favco (fishmonger), Anchorage, 12
fennel, in winter salad, 29
fiddleheads, with Alaska Game Skewers, 94, 95
fireweed, in idigenized cuisine, 86
fireweed honey, 76
fish broth (seafood fumet), 65–66
fish camp, 84
fisheries in Alaska, state constitution and sustainability, 60
fish heads, 44
Fish Stock, 53
 in Alaska Escabeche with Tzatziki, 11
 in Sitka Seafood Festival Chowder, 48
Flat Island community, 84
food
 indigenized, 84–87
 local, 2–3
 traditional, 3–4
food culture, importance of, 85–87
Foraged Fried Rice, 81
foraged items, washing, 70
Foraged Rice Pasta, 69–70
foraging, vii, 4
 See also produce, foraged
For the Rights of All: Ending Jim Crow in Alaska (documentary film), 15, 85

Fresh Alaska (web series), 78
Fresh Rolls with Herring Eggs, Sea Asparagus and Lovage, and Yarrow Dipping Sauce, 20–21
Frisch, Emma, 44, 46
fritters, 31
fry bread, history of, 110
Fry Bread with Labrador Tea and Cranberries, 110

game meat, 9
garlic, roasted
- in Bagna Cauda Vinaigrette, 51
- Roasted Garlic Puree, 50

granita, 22
Granny Smith apples, in winter salad, 29
Greek yogurt, in Tzatziki, 51
green beans, in Three Sisters Salsa, 38
griddle cakes, 31
grits, 36, 62

Haa Aani Oysterfest, Juneau, 22
Haa Aani Oysters Four Ways, 22–25
Hahn, Jennifer, 96
halibut cheeks, pan-seared, 75
herring eggs, in Fresh Rolls, 20
hijiki seaweed, 81
House-Made Salt Cod over Olive Oil Potatoes, 74
Howard Rock and Ted Stevens Smokehouse Gala, 86–87

Iced Chaga with Birch Syrup, 114
Indian ice cream, 108
Indian potatoes (troth), 103, 107
Indian Valley Meats, 102
indigenized food, 84–87

Kahiltna Birch Syrup, 113
Kahiltna Birchworks, Talkeetna, Alaska, 107
kale, 45, 75, 103
Kawerak Reindeer Herders Association, 90

Laborador Tea
- Fry Bread with Labrador Tea and Cranberries, 110
- in Tundra Vinaigrette, 70

lamb chops, Umpqua Valley, 98
linguine, Clams and Sausage in White Wine Broth, 72
local food, 2–3
lovage, 20
Lyons, Nancy, 57

macaroni and cheese, 99
Magnolia Grill, Durham, North Carolina, 50
Matanuska Valley, 8, 78
Matanuska Valley Carrot Puree, 96
meat and game
- Alaska Game Skewers with Alaska Berry-Birch Syrup Vinaigrette, 94–95
- Clams and Sausage in a White Wine Broth, 72
- Coffee-and-Creole-Spiced Reindeer Loin with Spruce-Tip Salt Finish, 90–91
- Elk Rolled Meatloaf, 92
- Moroccan-Spiced Umpqua Valley Lamb Chops over Matanuska Valley Carrot Puree and Spruce Tip Syrup, 96
- Noble's Delight, Featuring Alaska Reindeer, 99–101
- Red Beans and Rice with Reindeer Sausage, 102
- Wild Duck Risotto, 103

meat marinade, 94
Meyer Farms, 9
Meyers, Tim, 8
Midnite Sun Reindeer Ranch, Nome, 90
Montgomery, David, 56
moose, 99
Moroccan-Spiced Umpqua Valley Lamb Chops over Matanuska Valley Carrot Puree and Spruce Tip Syrup, 96
muktuk, 20
Muktuk Sushi Roll with Local Bean Sprouts, 27
mustard greens, 70

National Indian Health Board Culture Night (2011), 86, 108
National Museum of the American Indian (NMAI), Washington, D.C., 85
Native Youth Olympics, Anchorage, 32
Noble's Delight, Featuring Alaska Reindeer, 99–101
Noble's Diner, Anchorage, 102
NOLA restaurant, New Orleans, 91, 101
Nome, Alaska, 2, 90
Northern Polenta, 36
Norton Sound Economic Development Corporation (NSEDC), Nome, 15, 61
Norton Sound king crab, 61

Obama, Barack, 87
Olive Oil Potatoes, 41
- house-made salt cod and, 74

onions, caramelized, 101
Oysterfest, Juneau, 22
oysters, roasted, 25
oyster shooter or granita, 22
oyster shooter with alder-smoked salt rim and Alaskan summer ale, 23
oysters roasted with reindeer sausage and spinach, 25

Pacific Feast (Hahn), 96
palm trees of whale baleen and driftwood, 84
Pan-Seared Alaska Halibut Cheeks in a Birch–Brown Butter Sauce, served over Alaska Harvest Vegetable Tangle, 75
Pan-Seared Alaska Snow Crab–Stuffed Risotto Cakes with Winter Salad, 28–29
Pan-Seared Scallops with Ras El Hanout and Rosehip Vinaigrette, 76
Parsnip Cake with Spruce Tip Crema, 115

parsnips
- in Elk Rolled Meatloaf, 92
- in Parsnip Cake with Spruce Tip crema, 115
- in Roasted Root Veggies, 43
- in Toasted Quinoa-Root Vegetable Hash, 80

pasta
- Foraged Rice Pasta, 69–70
- linguine, with Clams and Sausage in White Wine Broth, 72
- rice noodles, 20, 69–70
- rice vermicelli, 44–45

pearl barley, 42
pesto, 49
Petersburg, Alaska, 2
pho, 44
Pickled Beet Vinaigrette, 79
pilot bread crackers, 32, 86
potatoes
- in Braised Rockfish with Fumet, 65–66
- in chowders, 46
- Dandelion Pesto Potatoes, 49
- Indian, 103
- in Matanuska Valley, 78
- Olive Oil Potatoes, 41, 74
- in Sitka Seafood Festival Chowder, 48
- Tlingit, 9

Princess Cruises, 19
produce, commercially grown
- apples, 12–13, 29
- bean sprouts, 27, 45
- beets, 19, 43, 79, 80
- cabbage, 13
- chard, 45
- cranberries, 95, 110
- cucumbers, 23, 27, 51
- fennel, 29
- green beans, 38
- kale, 45, 75, 103
- parsnips, 43, 80, 92, 115
- red onions, 31
- spinach, 25, 99
- squash, 20, 38, 103
- turnips, 45
- zucchini, 45, 75, 94
- *See also* carrots; potatoes

produce, foraged
- beach greens, 44, 70
- beach peas, 70
- bladderwrack seaweed, 81
- chaga, 107
- daikon radish, 43, 45, 81
- fiddleheads, 94, 95
- fireweed, 86
- lovage, 20
- sea/beach asparagus, 20, 27, 69–70, 81, 94, 95
- seaweed, 44, 65–66
- spruce tips, 86, 94
- troth (Indian potatoes), 107
- wormwood (stinkweed), 70
- yarrow, 21

quinoa-root vegetable hash, toasted, 80

"Ramp It Up: Skateboard Cultue in Native America" (NMAI exhibition), 85
Ras El Hanout Spice Blend, 77
Razor Clam Fritters, 31
razor clams, 72
Red Beans and Rice with Reindeer Sausage, 102
Red-Eye Gravy, 62
red salmon, 57
Red Wine Barley Risotto, 42
reindeer, 90, 99–101
reindeer sausage
- in Clams and Sausage in a White Wine Broth, 72
- oysters roasted with spinach and, 25
- red beans and rice with, 102
- in Sitka Seafood Festival Chowder, 48

resource protection, 4
rhubarb, 107
rhubarb, candied, 116
Rhubarb-Berry Agua Fresca, 116
Rhubarb Clafoutis with Whipped Spruce Tip Crema, 119
rice
- arborio, for risotto, 28, 42
- brown, in Foraged Fried Rice, 81
- brown, in Red Beans and Rice with Reindeer Sausage, 102
- brown, with Alaska Game Skewers, 94–95
- short grain, for sushi rolls, 27

rice noodles
- in foraged pasta, 69–70
- in fresh rolls, 20

rice paper, for fresh rolls, 20
rice vermicelli, in Alaska Salmon Head Pho, 44–45
risotto
- Pan-Seared Alaska Snow Crab–Stuffed Risotto Cakes, 28–29
- Red Wine Barley Risotto, 42
- Wild Duck Risotto, 103

Roasted Alaska Oysters, 23
roasted garlic, in Bagna Cauda Vinaigrette, 51
Roasted Garlic Puree, 50
Roasted Root Veggies, 43
rockfish, 65–66, 81
Roker, Al, cooking for, 86, 94

sable-fish, 74
Sailor Boy crackers, 32
salads
- Apple Slaw, 12–13
- Winter Salad, 29

salmon
- Alaska Salmon Head Pho, 44–45
- beet and vodka-cured gravlax, 19
- hand-crafted hot-smoked strips, 56
- over foraged rice pasta, 69–70
- pan-seared fillets, 45
- population of, 56–57
- Smoked Salmon White Bean Crostini, 32
- sockeye, from Bristol Bay, 12

Salmon with Pickled Beet Vinaigrette and Toasted Quinoa-Root Vegetable Hash, 78–80
salsa, 38
salt cod, house-made, 74
sauces
  Béarnaise Aioli, 15–16
  Béchamel Sauce, 100
  meat marinade, 94
  Red-Eye Gravy, 62
  Spruce Tip Crema, 115, 119
  Tzatziki, 11
  Yarrow Dipping Sauce, 21
scallops, pan-seared, 76
sea/beach asparagus
  with Alaska Game Skewers, 94, 95
  in Foraged Fried Rice, 81
  in fresh rolls, 20
  in muktuk sushi roll, 27, 69–70
seafood
  Alaska Escabeche with Tzatziki, 11
  Alaska King Crab Oscar Bites with Béarnaise Aioli, 15–16
  Alaska Oyster Shooter or Granita, 22
  Alaska Oyster Shooter with Alder-Smoked Salt Rim and Alaskan Summer Ale, 23
  Alaska Oysters Roasted with Reindeer Sausage and Spinach, 25
  Alaska Salmon Head Pho, 44–45
  Alaska Seafood Cakes with Apple Slaw, 12–13
  Arctic Shrimp and Grits with Bacon and Red-Eye Gravy, 62
  Beet and Vodka-Cured Alaska Salmon Gravlax, 19
  Braised Rockfish with Fumet, Vegetables, Seaweed, and Seal Oil, 65–66
  Bristol Bay Salmon over Foraged Rice Pasta and Tundra Vinaigrette, 69–70
  Clams and Sausage in a White Wine Broth, 72
  House-Made Salt Cod over Olive Oil Potatoes, 74
  Muktuk Sushi Roll with Local Bean Sprouts, 27
  Pan-Seared Alaska Halibut Cheeks in a Birch–Brown Butter Sauce, served over Alaska Harvest Vegetable Tangle, 75
  Pan-Seared Alaska Snow Crab–Stuffed Risotto Cakes with Winter Salad, 28–29
  Pan-Seared Scallops with Ras El Hanout and Rosehip Vinaigrette, 76
  red salmon, 57
  Roasted Alaska Oysters, 23
  Salmon with Pickled Beet Vinaigrette and Toasted Quinoa-Root Vegetable Hash, 78–80
  Seared Rockfish over Shrimp and Foraged Fried Rice, 81
  Sitka Seafood Festival Chowder, 48
  Smoked Salmon White Bean Crostini, 32
  whitefish, 108
seafood fumet (fish broth), 65–66
sea hunting tools, 85
Sealaska Corporation, 22
seal oil, 65–66
Seared Rockfish over Shrimp and Foraged Fried Rice, 81
seaweed, 81
  in Braised Rockfish with Fumet, Vegetables, Seaweed, and Seal Oil, 65–66
  fish head soup and, 44
shellfish stock, 52
shrimp
  Arctic Shrimp and Grits, 62
  Crab and Shrimp Stock, 52
  Seared Rockfish over Shrimp and Foraged Fried Rice, 81
side dishes
  Arctic Shrimp and Grits with Bacon and Red-Eye Gravy, 62
  Dandelion Pesto Potatoes, 49
  Olive Oil Potatoes, 41, 74
  Red Wine Barley Risotto, 42
  Roasted Garlic Puree, 50
  Roasted Root Veggies, 43
  Tzatziki, 51
Sitka, Alaska, 47
Sitka Farmers Market, 8
Sitka Seafood Festival, 46–47
Sitka Seafood Festival Chowder, 48
Smoked Salmon White Bean Crostini, 32
snow apple, in Alaska Salmon Head Pho, 45
snow machine with custom-made wagon, 60–61
sockeye salmon from Bristol Bay, about, 12
soups
  Alaska Salmon Head Pho, 44–45
  Chicken Stock, 53
  Corn Soup with Three Sisters Salsa, 38
  Crab and Shrimp Stock, 52
  Fish Stock, 53
  Sitka Seafood Festival Chowder, 48
spice blends
  Creole Spice (Bamnation!), 91
  ras el hanout, 77
spinach
  in Alaska Oysters Roasted with Reindeer Sausage and Spinach, 25
  in Noble's Delight, 99
spot shrimp, 62, 81, 86–87
Spruce Tip Crema, 115, 119
spruce tips
  in indigenized cuisine, 86
  in meat marinade, 94
spruce-tip sea salt, 90
Spruce Tip Syrup, 98
squash, in Corn Soup with Three Sisters Salsa, 38
sriracha sauce, 92
stocks, 52–53
subsistence foods, 3–4
subsistence lifestyle, 57, 86
sushi roll with muktuk and local bean sprouts, 27
sustainable fisheries, in constitution of Alaska, 60

Three Sisters Salsa, 38
Titus, Mark, 56
Tlingit artwork, Eagle clan, 86
"Tlingit bling" chef's jacket, 87
Tlingit potatoes story, 9
Toasted Quinoa-Root Vegetable Hash, 80
Totem Park, Sitka, 47
traditional food, 3–4
Traditional Foods, Contemporary Chef (video web series), 65, 87, 92, 103, 110
troth (Indian potatoes), 103, 107
tundra, 57
Tundra Vinaigrette, 70
turnips, in Alaska Salmon Head Pho, 45
Tyonek, Alaska, 8–9, 60
Tzatziki, 51
  escabeche with, 11

VanderWeeles, 78
vegetable stock, 52
  in Arctic Grits or Northern Polenta, 36
  in Clams and Sausage in a White Wine Broth, 72
  in Corn Soup with Three Sisters Salsa, 38
  in Noble's Delight, 99
  in Red Wine Barley Risotto, 42
vinaigrettes
  Alaska Rose Hip Vinaigrette, 76
  Bagna Cauda, 51
  Pickled Beet Vinaigrette, 79
  Tundra Vinaigrette, 70

Week of Healthy Living, Barrow, 27
white anchovies, in Bagna Cauda Vinaigrette, 51
white beans, in Smoked Salmon White Bean Crostini, 32
whitefish, 108
wild blueberries, picking, 2
Wild Duck Risotto, 103
Wild Rose Tea, 76
Williams, Noble, 47
Winter Salad, 29
wormwood (stinkweed), 70
Wounded Knee Skateboards and Propaganda, 85
Wrigley, Bryce and Jan, 36

Yarrow Dipping Sauce, 21

FINANCIAL SUPPORT PROVIDED BY

Bristol Bay Regional Seafood Development Association
Norton Sound Economic Seafood Development Association
Specialty Imports

THANKS GO TO

The King Career Center Culinary instructors, past, present and future.

Paul Ubl—photographer and teacher extrordinaire

Tom Yeakle, for teaching me how to roll with the punches

NOLA Restaurant, and the old school NOLA Rollas.

The CRUSH (Wine Bistro) Boys: Rob, Chad and Scott

The Noble's Diner Crew: Love you all

Mickey, Dan, Ma and Pa Neely

Tyonek Tribal Conservation District

National Museum of American Indian, DC

Dawn Biddison at the Smithsonian Arctic Studies Program

Jim "Murph" Murphy, Stronghold Society

Wounded Knee Skateboards

Alaska Native Tribal Health Consortium

National Indian Health Board

Southeast Alaska Regional Health Consortium

First Alaskans Institute

Sealaska Corporation

Haa Aani

CIRI Foundation

Ketchikan Indian Community

Tundra Womens Coalition

Yupiit School District

First Light

Anna Hoover

Pamyua

Rasmuson Foundation

Alaska Public Media

Alaska Seafood Marketing Institute

Sitka, for being Sitka

ANTHC Diabetes health and wellness team

University Alaska Fairbanks Cooperative Extension

Alaska Food Policy Council

Alaska Humanities Forum

Kawerak Reindeer Herding Association

Midnite Sun Reindeer Ranch

Alaska Pure Sea salt

Kahiltna Birch Syrup

Steam dot coffee

Alaska Sprouts

Alaska Flour Company

Van Whye Family Farm

Mat Valley Meats/Butcher Block no 9

AD Farms, Rempel Family Farm, Vanderweele Farm Meyer Farm

And all the other hardworking farmers, harvesters and producers of beautiful Alaska foods in the Last Frontier.

Alaska Grown, Division of Agriculture, State of Alaska

Ash Adams and Brian Adams

Kristi Trimmer

Emma Frisch

Mark Titus

David Montgomery

James Fraioli

Jennifer Hahn

The Bear Trail Lodge

My Family—Terri June (Mom), RJK1 (dad), John, Scot, Sara, Jessie, and Robin.

Special thanks to Ret. Col Perry, and Rita Nuhn for all your support, and raising an amazing daughter.

THE CIRI FOUNDATION

This project is funded in part by The CIRI Foundation

Alaska Native chef Rob Kinneen is out to revolutionize how Alaskans eat by bringing together local ingredients and contemporary cooking. Beyond the Arctic Polenta and Razor Clam Fritters with Smoked Mustard Aioli, the *Fresh Alaska Cookbook* will provide resources for Alaskan and non-Alaskan cooks who want to taste more of the flavors unique to the state. Kinneen describes the culinary culture of the many regions and peoples of Alaska and argues for the importance of a local food movement. Salmon, crab, and moose figure prominently in the book, of course, but so do updates of foods like agudak. From coast to interior, Alaska never tasted so good!

CHEF ROBERT KINNEEN was born in Petersburg, Alaska. He is of Native Alaska Tlingit heritage and has been working in restaurants since he was 15 years old. Rob attended the Culinary Institute of America in Hyde Park, New York. He has worked and staged in Alaska, Illinois, Louisiana, New York, and North Carolina.

Rob is currently a chef and runs a catering company in Durham, North Carolina where he lives with his wife Carolyn, their daughter Sylvie, and her dog brother Elliott.

ASH ADAMS is a photojournalist based in Anchorage, Alaska who specializes in environmental portraiture and documentary. Adams' work has been featured in *The New York Times*, *The Guardian*, *The Wall Street Journal*, *The Washington Post*, *Rolling Stone*, *The Alaska Dispatch News*, *Aljazeera America*, and other national and international publications.

BRIAN ADAMS is an editorial and commercial photographer based in Anchorage, Alaska specializing in environmental portraiture and medium-format photography. His work has been featured in both national and international publications, and his work documenting Native Alaska villages has been showcased in galleries across the United States. His first book of photography, *I AM ALASKAN*, was published in October 2013 by University Of Alaska Press. His most recent book, *I AM INUIT,* was published in December 2017.

COOKING
UNIVERSITY OF ALASKA PRESS

SNOWY OWL BOOKS

PRINTED IN CANADA

$40.00
ISBN 978-1-60223-359-1
54000>
9 781602 233591